© Copyright 2024 by Sharon Francis - All rights reserved.

The moral rights of the author have been asserted.

© Copyright 2024 Cover Artwork & Interior Artwork by Sharon Francis
No artwork is to be copied or duplicated.

It is not legal to reproduce, duplicate or transmit any part of this book in either electronic or photographic means, recording or printed format.

Recording of this publication in any form is strictly prohibited,
Without prior written permission of the author.

ISBN 978-1-7385171-1-4 First Edition

Contact Information: outsmart@lysgworld.co.uk
Website: lysgworld.com

Publisher: LYSGworld

This book is dedicated to
All the Captive Souls on The Earth Dimension
And Beyond
Spirit Housed in Physical Body

For Rochelle and Molly

# TWO FUCKERS PLAYING CHESS USING US AS THE PAWNS!
### THE EGO IS A NARCISSIST

## Breaking Away From The Entity That Controls You
By Sharon Francis

# Table of Contents

Introduction

The Journey Inwards

**Principle One**....................................................4

**Principle Two**....................................................11

**Principle Three**..................................................20

**Principle Four**...................................................23

**Principle Five**....................................................30

**Principle Six**.....................................................37

**Principle Seven**.................................................48

**Principle Eight**..................................................54

**Principle Nine**...................................................62

**Principle Ten**.....................................................75

**Principle Eleven**.................................................86

**Carrying Another's Cross**.....................................89

**Realisation Before It's Too Late**...........................92

**Other Worlds**....................................................105

**Principle Twelve**................................................117

**Principle Thirteen**..............................................127

Principle Fourteen..................................................133

Principle Fifteen....................................................140

Principle Sixteen...................................................150

Principle Seventeen................................................156

Going Even Deeper................................................178

Epilogue (1)..........................................................187

Epilogue (2)..........................................................189

Last Words...........................................................190

Acknowledgments................................................191

The Author

# 𝕴ntroduction

This isn't some run-of-the-mill book, it is actually Exceptional! My intention is to share what I've experienced and learnt in order to give you the 'Process', the way out (both sides permitting). I'm actually being driven to write this, so, subject to requirements, could even say a calling to bring some truth into this place we call earth, or rather 'The Earth Dimension' or you can call it what you like, who cares, it's just a name… however, it does have its origins but for now that isn't important! So, for argument sake, let's just say it's where we think we are at the moment… 'Moment' being the operative word. Soon you'll understand that life on earth has all been a ritualistic farce, amongst other things. An un funny joke – a hoax at the cost of losing our fucking minds, and the ability to independently think for ourselves, a hoax at our expense - one big Game of Chess, with backdrops consisting of illusion or rather ILLUSIONS! One being 'We Don't Die, We come back', – and No, I'm not talking about reincarnation! Also, there is 'No' Heaven or Hell, although where we are is questionable!

I'm about to walk You through 'Your Dark' and put the 'Light On', I may seem to repeat certain things - that is because there is no one way to explain what is contained within this book.

So, Buckle Up and Enjoy the Ride!

# The Journey Inwards

You have to walk from A to B To find
out what A means.

On your way along the road, The
wolves will come out Appearing on
each side of you, You will stop
walking
Because you think they will get you.

But if you carry on walking,
You will see that they are tied up And can
only come out so far.

You will then discover that They were
just an illusion
To stop you from completing your journey.


We are Spirit Housed in a Physical Body Existing on a Physical Plane.
Our Mission - to Get Home!

I have always known that I am here to do Something.

What I thought it was; it wasn't And was never going to be.

However, from that, I figured out how to 'Be'

Until I became who I Am.

# Principle {1}

Ok, where the fuck do I start... People who think they are (woke) awake, aren't even awake, you need to be awake within your woke to become awake. Laugh because I am!

You can't just clear out your past issues and indoctrinations and think you've done it. No! There's more to it! I did that and shit still kept happening, like continuing to attract situations and people into my life that I thought would've gone as a result of the work I had done on myself. I faced, accepted and relinquished the attachments to my past, along with automatic behavior and thoughts all cyclic in nature, me unaware of being a constructed self or rather - a sheep. I had to learn how to stop something that sounded like me from dictating what it wanted me to be, in order to become who, I am, – which in all fairness I always was! I didn't know it but they did..."who's they? you may ask", not necessarily my family, although they had been instrumental in assuring that I stayed docile for as long as I did, like every family does. Holding their children hostage to an indoctrinated set of standards, programmed into them as a form of ideals that they don't even know the origin of. Yes, but No... I'm talking about an energy, a guiding force that resides on our planet, I will call it 'The Custodian', the entity who likes to think and command that it is the only ultimate power that exists - although Not True! It needs for us to believe it... however, it is a power to be reckoned with, as the majority are controlled by it. Although a vibration - it is experienced as physical in form pertaining to wants and needs, but sadistic in its execution. By the way I need to add, that through its arrogance will not allow me to portray it in any other way! 'The Beautiful Being' that it is... I say beautiful out of respect for the way it has cleverly and successfully constructed a world of its own, where humanity as its subjects have forgotten who they are, where they come from, and what they continuously do, to assure they stay that way, has certainly been 'Beautifully' done! Therefore, I introduce the 'Visible!' henceforth the 'Physical Exterior Force'... Ta Da!

We are living or rather occupying a physical plane of existence. It is physical because we can see it and touch it, manipulate it and kill things in it (or so we think).

The majority don't believe what they cannot see; some people don't believe a thing or situation exists unless it happens to them. The majority collectively fear the same thing, the majority collectively hate the same thing, the majority collectively love the same thing, or should I say what they believe to be 'Love!' Or is it just human physical desire i.e. lust? Think about it, because the love here seems to be subject to many conditions, for example, race, colour, cast, ethnicity, what you can give, what you have got, along with, what you can do for someone etc. The list goes on, there are many love languages... however, I can assure you love as we know it (IS NOT LOVE) or Loving! With that said, all the above is a distraction - People seem to be easily swayed, manipulated and thus controlled. To begin with, the mainstream media at this point remains a physical entity on our planet, that the majority plug themselves into in one way or another (through guided habit) – or rather, it plugs into them. Going deeper, – it is part of an ordered construct to keep things in line, or rather, 'You' in line! With its marginalised influences, news which is constructed, contrived and directed, then distributed, containing the preferences of a small handful of people who have financial ownership over it, investment, and or interest in the concealment of facts that are of public interest, in order to sensor and control the narrative they desire the people to ingest. Along with leaders who present no better than the ones before, solving only to tighten the reigns around the necks of humanity rather than represent them. For only one purpose, well, two, actually three - mass control, concealment of their own shit, and money, a privilege only the few seemingly manage to obtain... albeit at a price nonetheless! I will call that 'The Contract'... Which brings me back to the 'Beautiful Being', the rather clever 'Custodian'.

The Faustian Bargain, - the contract, is afforded to those with influence, to the entertainers but not limited to just them, as it reaches across the board to whomever has obtained high popularity. Undoubtably, by imposing on our interest, - from so called royalty, politicians, inventors, sports men and women, owners and investors of large corporations, who cream off the tops of their franchised brands, multi-billionaires and so on… the contract pertains to a trade made with the custodian for full rights to one's soul, with the life force that resides within it. To command and order as it wishes, in-keeping with its own agenda. This contract permits the custodian to silence the influential and use them to assist in the brainwashing and manipulation of the masses (bear with me) - in return for worldwide presence and money, I won't say genuine power because they lost that the moment they succumbed to the contract, however, I will say; and concealment of succumbed to misdemeanours and temptations of unlawful cravings, which hang over their heads as leverage, if they choose to breach the agreement. Haven't you noticed that so called famous people don't ever have much of an opinion with regards to what goes on in our world? Whether it be right or wrong? Unless they are touting the cleverly constructed agenda of the custodian, to further sink you. If they do speak they seem to end up dead, endure harsh humiliation or portrayed in the media as crazy, losing their shit! This is no coincidence.

The Contract demands they keep a loyal silence! Reminding them through fuck knows what means, that it's what they signed up for! Unless they are willing to give up all benefits received in the exchange! Which will be undeniably costly to them! With that said, the trade will not be easily withdrawn whilst on the physical plane, not even through physical death. For 'them', I am assured that the soul may never make it home, but just receives constant winning tickets back to an illusionary dimension to be re- programmed, where their life force can be propelled into harvesting, stored as backup for the Custodian to later distribute in aid of further mass control and chaos... thus wealth and untold riches be the trap of the influential famous physical being, along with delusions of grandeur - which for some reason the masses pander to. Strange isn't it? because in all truthful reality, no one is better than, or more important than anyone else! bearing in mind we are souls housed in a physical body, - I'd like to say having an enjoyable earthly experience! Not! Come on its funny shit though! People continue to be duped by who they believe to be more superior to them, hanging off their every word, trying to follow what they do, and doing what they are told, both through spoken word and subliminally.

As cattle we chew their chaff, allowing ourselves to be herded to go in a certain direction. Whilst at the same time our energy is being stolen and harvested, through the very attention we choose to give... The majority of the collective state of minds live in fear; for one reason or another! You have been deliberately driven there and you don't even know it! Are you aware binary frequencies that you are sensitive to, have been placed within the body of music, that specific artists who have been headhunted for stardom use. It is having an effect on you likened to the mesmerising pull of the pied piper of Hamelin! as it manipulates you into supporting them, or rather worshipping them? Along with visuals, the negative coding is imbedded in the frequency, the words carry the spell, the message within the song. The vibration travels directly to your psyche, aided by its repetition of the song. You will recognise this all too well- the times you've heard a song for the first time and not really liking it, to then after, being repeatedly bombarded with it, you find yourself singing along with it! All the while you are being hypnotized by the frequency hidden within the music! Along with the symbols and subliminal messages contained within tv adverts and advertising, including billboards and not to mention the radio waves circulating around us from the satellites in the sky that currently sit above our heads... and dare I add chemical trails! At this point I won't even mention the amped up phone mast frequencies! Inventing viruses to cause disorders and disease, then insisting on drugging us all to our own detriment in the name of social inclusion! Billions of dollars were amassed with that one...

That's when they are not busy sexualising everybody including the children, encouraging lust as the point of affection, instead of Love! We are all being absolutely 'Fucked over' and don't even know it!

# Principle {2}

Your existence is on repeat, whilst your 'Sense of Self' deteriorates. Different situations, same characters, nothing changes. Over and over like bloody ground hog day, then your body grows old and you sort of die! Ever heard the saying 'set in your ways' not having lived? Well, you've definitely been 'SET!' Your aspirations seem to be, to go on holiday a few times a year, and own your own home and cars etc.… that seems to be it in a nutshell, – oh, and own your own bloody holiday home! That seems to be what you measure your worth on… the material goods you can amass before you die. Most of you work your arses off then die before you can even enjoy what you've worked so bloody hard for, the question is then: what was the fucking point? Again, it's another distraction!

You busy yourselves conforming to rules and regulations - I say again! Worshiping those in the entertainment business – royal family's and politicians, those who you believe worthy to have power and influence over you, evidently because you must think them better than you? Have you ever asked yourself what actually makes them any different from you? What do they actually do for you? How do they actually make you feel? Entertained? Because from where I'm sitting they seem to glorify a standard of living that you believe you could never attain... I guess that makes them worthy of your attention and your money then! What you are really being guaranteed is, that on some level within yourself - they are making you feel less than them! It's strange how you derive pleasure from parking your exhausted self in front of a box, transfixed on whoever or rather, 'whatever' is on the screen, mesmerised by them. Then an advert comes up and you're then influenced by that... please reflect on that. Now the question is: what would you sell your soul for? Because unbeknownst to you, in one way or another we sell off parts of our selves every day 'For Free!' No bartering or deals we just freely give it up... by being compliant to the rules and wishes of others without question - to others who are exterior to ourselves. Our attentions are directed outside of ourselves towards everything and everyone but ourselves. Your sense of what you deem important is displaced. Another distraction another requirement of the Custodian.

Have you ever looked at yourself in the mirror, and I mean, really looked at yourself? Into your own eyes? or noticed that you have ears, a face, the texture of your skin, your mouth, your nose…? I remember when I first looked at me, or rather saw 'Me', I actually felt uncomfortable, because a feeling came back at me, it took a while before I could gaze into my eyes without looking away. Upon inspecting me, and getting used to the feeling rising from within me, I can now say that what I was feeling, is what I know now to be my energy life force - my vibration. I was royally shocked the day I noticed my hands, that I have hands and what they do for me, along with my hair that has grown beautifully for me. You ask, 'why is she talking about seeing her body'? Strange as it seems, and although we live inside it, many of us don't really regard it or pay attention to it, well not really. We may dress it and put make-up on it, shoes, and underwear on to it to enable it to walk around outside, and feed it! Then bury it when it stops working in whatever way that may be? Other than that, we don't really give a shit about it or what it does for us from day-to-day… except to notice when it's out of shape or when it gets spots, when its hair drops out or doesn't look the way we want it to, and all pertaining to what? What we see in the media, or should I say what we have compared it to in the media, - believing that if it doesn't match then it isn't worthy. Look at all the shit out there being sold, potions and lotions, stuff in needles that people are using to alter the face, why! Because so called famous people do it, some people's faces don't even look real anymore. The once 'Absolutely Beautiful', end up looking like botched up caricatures! But you still do it! - Lost! you want to look like them, 'when they don't even want to look like themselves!'

You want to look like everyone else but yourselves! You want to be like everyone else but Your-Selves! What really needs to be considered is who set the standard for what you should look like in the first place, standards with mental tick-able boxes? Boxes that reside in your head, judgments that are once again exterior, otherwise you would pay no attention to the body.

Have you ever listened to what you think, have you even noticed that you have an inner dialogue, ever stopped to hear it? I guess as you don't pay attention to your body you're not going to pay attention to your fucking mind are you! We need to be aware of what we are thinking - what we believe, or rather what our beliefs are on an unconscious level, as opposed to or compared to what we consciously think our beliefs to be. One is the ego, what we've been told, indoctrinated and programmed to believe, - it has always been exterior to us, designed to contradict our 'True' truth. We are not here to just live or rather, exist for a time then Die! The truth is: We are not here in our rightful capacity, we are 'Spirit' occupying a physical body having a physical experience. We have not become aware of this, and as a result we have ended up as a programmed construct, a 'False Self'. We pay no attention to the environment we personally occupy, in any given moment, for instance the street, shopping centre or mall as we walk through it.

The detail, is where I'm going with this, as what we choose to notice along with what we are thinking at the time, can warrant a completely different perception, thus experience. For instance, – two people could walk down the same road at exactly the same time and see different things, or rather, notice different things, through choice I might add! Why is that? That's because they are housing different perceptions pertaining to the life they live or have lived. For example, one could notice that it's a sunny day, blue sky and see birds, whereas the other could see shit on the ground, junk that someone has left, and think the sun beating down on them is too much to bear! Albeit whilst walking down the exact same road at the exact same time. Whichever way it is seen, the point I'm making is; what is noticed all comes from how the person chooses to perceive it. What makes their experience (perceptions) different? I am inclined to look at what is going on in the mind of each person, at that precise moment as they walk, - the thoughts and the emotion, that encompass, the thought it accompanies. Thoughts carry a vibration, although mostly undetected, noticed, or heard, - how they all tie to what you experience are relative to the outcome. How things are observed and seen physically, entices the question, where does this energy go if not comprehended or sensed? Chosen as a way in which to taste the world around you - It stays secular and stores itself in the outer body as a memory, to inject into your life experience as a belief, depending on what you resonate with in the story. Energy is fluid, it never dissolves it just transmutes.

You have become passive - a victim or rather a person with a victim mentality. This has happened unconsciously; your barely audible thoughts create beliefs that become energy based. Alive, they become your truth, thus, need to seek confirmation of their existence to survive and thrive. In order to do this - the energy attracts more of the same, as in situations and people. When validated, the energy within the notion of the belief, grows stronger within the person. Basically, the more you think of a thing, the more you will become drawn to it or, draw it to you like a magnet. The more you experience it, - the more it becomes enmeshed as 'Your Truth'. The more it becomes your truth, the more the need for it to be experienced! Stray thoughts beliefs and trauma are debris that take away your focus, and ability to manifest different outcomes for yourself. When the stray thoughts are accompanied by feeling and emotion, they become spells that come into being! If you believe the notions and traumas to be your true state of mind they will become your beliefs! They will be "What you end up seeing and experiencing life through!" Any separate want, need or positive affirmation, will become opposition to what you already deem a belief. It will then become trapped by the debris of what is already there. Instead what becomes manifest and affirmed are the existing notions and beliefs. The new wants get stuck in the current mess, because the current mess (debris) is stronger due to repetition, older, and more potent, as it has existing memory attached to it, hence! that is why you manifest Not what is wanted but 'More' of what is 'Not!' you will only get what is already attached to the dominant thoughts that are already there, their existence has been dependent on the attention you give to them!

The effect on your mind will leave you to believe your life is going around in circles, and thinking that nothing you try ever works… It 'can't!' because you don't really believe it will! Your unconscious shadows (debris) won't let you! They have never been consciously released or even detected, they exist by constantly manifesting as your reality. No matter how much effort, or positivity you put into an affirmation, desire, or the doing of a thing, whether to get something better, or a different outcome in life. Because of existing debris, – it will 'Never' happen. Then you'll just put it down to bad luck, or say it's not the right time, or whatever shit you normally say to yourself when something doesn't work out for you… its 'Not' bad luck its 'You!' preventing anything new because of your shadows! The newness gets stuck in the Oldness, in fact the newness gets obliterated dissolved and shot down by your existing debris! It's like they lay in wait, then pounce as soon as you have a positive thought. Always in objection… the stray thought will come in and say 'No' You Won't', destroying what you've just tried to manifest. Remember this - thoughts are energy. 'Spells!'… 'No, you won't!' is going to be the strongest because it has been fueled by you for the longest, so it will be the result you will get. 'The Secret' never told you that bit did it! Now you know why affirmations don't bloody work! Self- analyses, is the only way out. Becoming aware of what you believe on a subconscious level, becoming aware of your shadows, and viewing them as little voices on repeat, having awareness of them will dissipate the influence they have over you.

However, if you choose to experience them as just another uncomfortable feeling, you 'Will' be left in denial! ignorant and blinded to what is really taking place and happening to you. That's how our thoughts work, like spell casting, with 'You' as your own witch, 'Hocus Pocusing' your-self! As it has become your truth your thought and belief, naturally you will attract situations and experiences attuned to its vibration - thus! Experiencing only that, will follow.

'Through our Perceptions, Accordingly, we 'Will' See!'

So, we have free will to choose what we think, or do we? The answer is in fact Yes! However, because we are sponge-like, the answer is No! We are being assailed, us not being mindful, or even aware that we have a mind, or that it can, and does absorb naturally; has assured that we pick up all kinds of influences, ideology's and indoctrinations that have driven us to believe them into being our reality. Our beliefs are like programmes which live in the unconscious part of ourselves, they determine who and what we see reflected back to us in the exterior - the mirror! - how we feel about ourselves, how we live, what we experience and how we are treated. Many of our beliefs come from the foundation our parents or carers laid, bestowed upon us in the form of standards and values. The way they do things and the way they feel about things pertaining to what they believed about themselves, further based on how they were raised, treated and nurtured, or not.

The opportunities they had and how far they got in life, which they normally judged by how much material wealth they managed to amass. All of the above are tied to self-worth or the lack of! They influenced us with how we see ourselves, however, somebody influenced them, but how did they influence them? Who influenced those before them and so on and so forth! Or rather, What influenced them? You see everything and everyone through the filters of what you already believe, what you have been indoctrinated with, including the 'Media!' and last but not least the influencers, entertainers the ones who sold their souls to the fucking custodian! assisting in joyfully 'Famously' keeping you stuck in the Matrix! 'The Programme!' feeding from your unrealised 'Shadow'. So, do we really have Free Will? No because we are being manipulated, and Yes! If we wake up!

Duality is Yin and Yang, Shadow, the absence of Light, Positive and Negative, Interior World, Exterior World, God the Infinite Creator of All, and the Devil, which if spelt backwards is 'Lived`, so contains Duality within itself! As people generally think of death when the devil is mentioned or some sort of dark shit! God the Unseen and Devil the Seen! Spiritual and Physical, In and Out. They are all Dualities! Opposites of each other. Balance: we can't experience The One without having experienced The Other, likened to; the truth of 'We Wouldn't know What Good is, if there wasn't Bad'. It is what you are 'Not' aware of, what you 'Don't' know that keeps you trapped! Affirmations do not clear negative thoughts and beliefs - 'Hearing' them 'Out' does!

# Principle {3}

From a young age I was taught not to listen to myself, not to trust myself, what I saw, or even pay attention to what I hear, which was confusing, because my parents, or rather the people who cared for me, would often lie and not admit to things that happened, in the way they happened, and the part they played in contributing to said happening. Family dynamics, became all about passing the energy of blame, and wrong doing onto one another, or the one they could successfully make feel and carry guilt the most. This allowed them to alleviate themselves as the perpetrator, from feeling anything, or taking any responsibility or fault, thus enabling them to bounce unaffected through another day! To continue aiding the custodian programming.

So, what happens to the person that has been filled with guilt? They are left drained and heavy. Mentally they are in victim mode, continually used as the scapegoat; fucked up shit right! Likened to how a vampire drains blood to feed... this is 'Energy Vampirism'. I'll call it Energy Exchange, it goes like this: Their negative vibration, energy is passed on to you, as they syphon yours! through inflicting fear or some other unwanted emotion, passively or aggressively. The outcome will be guilt, but mostly towards yourself, – as they have cleverly attached it to something you already believe, so therefore you think it true! Guilt is the favourite as it has the power to sneak up on its receiver. It is extremely manipulative, thus bearing plenty of fruit for the initiator, assuring substantial returns of stolen power, the energy and life force of another. We do this to each other in many ways. At work through position hierarchy, perceived opportunities that have been built up and promised then sold to us (like an insurance policy) just so we could invest our energy of attention. All to discover that the opportunity didn't really exist, and was always going to lead to nothing but a false investment in hope. Your investment, being the energy feed for the instigator. Declarations of love as in 'Love Bombing', false gestures of compassion and friendship, a narcissistic favourite. Then there is manipulative information, whether it's pertaining to one person, or a narrative, that is specifically fed to every person, pertaining to the influence of a deception that the media decides to spew out in order to keep mass thought under control. All led in a direction beneficial to the few who have most to gain, which is 'Never' the people... and it goes on.

What these all have in common is, they need and require another's validation, along with attention. With regards to the media, politicians and so-called royalty, their success is due to the mass perception, being, a huge lack of self-worth, not desiring to stand alone in our endeavours, and each person giving over full responsibility of themselves, - albeit to their own detriment. Over time it will become prevalent that these influencers did not have our best interests at heart. What others say to us, and get away with doing to us, is all based on what we individually believe about ourselves on an unconscious level. Our intuition has been clouded, blocked with false perceptions – that we believed to be the truth, believing there is no alternative! Trusting that what we have been told is our only point of reference, we became comfortable and mentally lazy.

# Principle {4}

Spiritual Warfare. The attack on our soul is a real thing! Two elements at loggerhead, - one using us as its weapon for superior control of our energy and destiny, and the other wanting us to keep our energy, feel love, power and freedom. This has nothing to do with skin colour, shape or form, it is to do with power! Inner power - our energy force. Spiritual being, versus the outer physical, the custodian entity uses our lack of personal material wealth to control. Material wealth equals to what is perceived here as power. I will say it again; We are spirit housed in a physical body existing (just) on a physical plane. Nothing is as it seems, everything is the opposite to what it really is! Nothing is real here except Energy, Vibration.

We believe we are the body because it is what we can touch, it has sensations, with a head, that has eyes that can see, and ears, that can hear, a mouth to eat - with sound that comes out of it, so we can verbally communicate through it. However, we only have a body because it is our vehicle, to get about whilst being on this physical plane vibration. What we don't know is that we control it through our spirit, life force, our consciousness.

Everything here is experienced as solid to the touch. So, it makes sense, that in order to fit in with the solid - a body was created, a functional body, thought manifest into physical reality. The custodian being an expression of the creative force, needed it that way. But in order for these bodies to work they needed life force inside of them. For argument sake, a life force born of both dark, on the outside, and light on the inside, - Yin and Yang - encompassing both energies - light transmutable once it has determined where it truly belongs. I use those two definition words, light and dark to simplify, as they are majority recognised descriptions. I say dark as in void of the knowledge of where it originally came from, thus in the dark unable to see or perceive, - and light as in recollection of its origin, thus illuminated, – to see with full perception. Until we as energy become transmuted, we remain captured, and re-harvested by the custodian; to sustain and ensure the ongoing repetition of this physical existence.

Our energy, becomes stored to be born again into another body, held by attachments, incurred from the experiences had, whilst being in the dark, as the attachment relates more to that existence. Because the energy of the attachment relates more to that existence (believes it is Reality) It makes sense that it would come back, because it wouldn't belong anywhere else but within the physical realm. As our consciousness is shadowed by it, we have No choice than to be dragged along with it. Until we transmute and dissipate attachment to all physical form, and become aware that they are 'Not; (our truth) in relation to the physical planes. Until we become custodians' harvesters of our own energy life force, - We will not be permitted or able to go home.

Through false ideologies, free will, fear, manipulation and lust. The custodian traps us and leads us to believe that we as people (not souls) need something to believe in, other than ourselves. This is true from the standpoint of not having been aware of the soul, the self. However, because we hold both energies, there has to be duality, so truth runs concurrent at all times. Books were written containing partial truths, cloaked truths, deceptive truths, most made to sound crazy or outlandish, whilst needing to make a semblance of sense, relating to what we had experienced pertaining to the souls voyage. Monuments that appear impossible for a human to have built (that's because they didn't). Some built to provide nostalgia, as we crave to feel a sense of home, we incorrectly seek it in old ruins, some to keep us curious enough to search, whilst at the same time, remaining distracted by our attachments.

Hieroglyphs depicting stories, and scenes of another world existence, from wherever the fuck knows. Not forgetting movies, all films are designed to keep us in limbo, – stuck, in one way or another, – whether that be in a certain mindset or emotion. One example, to obvious Not to mention; black people, now a faction, faction 1, will know all too well, of the mainstream films that depict them as subordinates, having mindsets of low intelligence, slavery films that are not only repressive but regressive, - an attachment, cleverly engineered by the custodian, through its owned minions (black and white directors and producers), to ensure, the minds of the 'color-Full' stays rooted in the sense of inferiority, whilst the other factions look on! I will call them faction 2, for the sake of this section. Oblivious to the notion of the same plan being used on them! just in a different way, and in fact even more sinister and dark. Faction 2, you have been brainwashed into feigning superiority (received as an attachment), 'unconscious or otherwise', which derives from the scriptures written in the bible, stating, 'So God created man in his own image, in the image of God, created he him', and, (this is the sinister part) those with influence, seized it as an opportunity, to assure that the accompanying artwork to be held in reverence, was of a white god!. Hasn't anybody ever wondered, even a little, who cooked that one up? I guess not, - Now! on the strength of the artwork… faction 2, being that you bear a resemblance to the sketched god; albeit deliberately set up that way, it had been used as an opportunity for you to be regarded as the superior race! What's even more dark is the majority believed it!

There are 'No' physical representations for God the most High! Because it is an Energy! a Vibration! The same energy and vibration, that resides within us all. Spirit has No colour! That is what makes us all the same! you can't just draw a picture and say its GOD! Who the fuck does that! Creating visuals to represent a so-called lord god that looks like them, deliberately, in order to give the entity in them power and entitlement over other factions. There should've 'Never' been any factions in the first place! Lack of Self-awareness and opportunity led faction 2, to disregard what is actually written: God created man in His 'Own' image', 'Not 'One' Image!'... Not that one has to read that to know that! considering 'Man' is made up of different 'races, and ethnicities!'. Like I said earlier, the truth always has to run concurrent to the lie, in order to create Balance! I guess that bit was left in for that reason, before they fucked about with the rest of it. These statements accompanied by the artwork (sketched by a man) were then distributed, and preached around the world to all races and ethnicities to be accepted as fact! The majority in those times and now, enjoyed the conditioning of privilege so much, along with all the historical wickedness endured by the other faction, that somewhere along the way you lost your fucking minds! However, The distraction of this attachment, has solidified your place in the custodians world, to be used as its fodder, along with the others who are asleep.

Faction 2, fooled into believing the shade of your skin is the preference of God, a gift, when in reality the only gift you will get, is a ticket back here, or to one of many dimensional existences that you have created. Factions 1, and 2, if not realised and dissipated! your belief in both the attachment of 'inferiority', and 'superiority' will prevent (Both Factions) from becoming aware of 'Self ' and returning home!

One of 'Your' lessons faction 2, is to see beyond the colour of skin! No 'ONE' has privilege over another!

Faction 2, your fear of faction 1, originates from unconsciously projecting aggressions that you refuse to see in yourselves. These aggressions are the consequences of 'You' having been conditioned, tricked into sacrificing your own power to the custodian, they are 'Your' reflections of resentment! albeit hidden from you. By believing superiority and privilege to be your truth, the awareness of your own creative power has been blocked, harnessed by the custodian. Remember, our energy is the true currency here! Whilst at the same time, faction 1, has been conditioned to believe they are inferior, thus blocking their awareness of having any power at all! – when in actual fact, your power has just been lain dormant.

Faction 2, Your fear is in fact, of your own denied power, being reflected back at you through faction 1. Instead of sensing it as that, you are choosing to experience faction 1, as 'threatening', because you are being blinded by your own projections!

With that said, this is the very clever trick of the custodian, deliberately placed in you, as an attachment, to prevent you from becoming aware of your same-ness, meaning, the aspects of yourself in faction 1.

This has also been cleverly done to keep faction 1, on the vibration of resentment, both unconscious and conscious, towards faction 2. The root of the resentment in faction 1, originates from faction 2, projecting the aggressions they refuse to see in themselves onto faction 1. Your lesson here Faction 1, is to Realise, thus integrate, and 'Remember', that you are Powerful beings, Energy! who have been 'Conditioned' to believe you are the opposite. In truth, 'You' are 'Spirit' housed in physical vessel! 'Your' power 'Will' be brought into your existence if 'You' become 'Aware of Self!'

The custodian knows, power over 'All' as pawns, will be lost if we remember what we are. Its task is to ensure we don't! "Do you see it?" We have been Deceived into Believing in Difference! We, like 'Pawns' in a game of Chess, the custodian entity has Brilliantly maneuvered us around the board, using your lack of Self-Awareness as the fuel to do it!

Colour of skin is insignificant! 'Not' important! The measure and weight of the heart is! judgement is weighed by your intent. We are all part of the same Creative Power! Albeit on different vibrations, Spirit has No colour! Meaning, when we attack others, we are really attacking ourselves.

Anyway… all films are designed to keep us in limbo, – stuck in one way or another, whilst at the same time containing truths for us to decipher if we are awake! This is all dependant on whether we have managed to tap into our spiritual (illuminated) side. To be honest the only truths we ever needed has always been contained within us. With that said, unfortunately people can't be arsed to look for any truths, they rather fuck about down here, then die, and then come the fuck back…to end up deader, denser and more severed from Self, than when they left!

# Principle {5}

Whilst trying to write this section of the book, I am being tested with many distractions, undesirable people from my past are showing up, wanting to be close friends again. Guys I had gone on a date with, who were no good for me, are showing up and offering me themselves, whereas before they gave no time, unless they were guaranteed there would be something in it for them. Anyway, I realised that as soon as I engage with them, I lose my flow of energy, the energetic enthusiasm that brings me the words to write, my mind goes blank, direction ceases. Along with, when I do read through what I've already written, in an attempt to remind myself - I don't understand what I'm reading, as if I've been blindfolded; shut out of my own room, and thus prevented access to my own knowledge and wisdom. It's like becoming cast out on to a lower vibration! Scary shit isn't it!

So, I now realise that the only way I can bring myself back on track with full understanding, is to write what's happening to me as it's happening. To ground myself I am required to become the observer (like a fly on the wall in my own life) and let go of these fuckers that are trying to fuck with me, (as I laugh) and in relief, I have you know! Only because I've found the doorway out! The process is 'Real' people! So, what happened to me is: through giving attention to another, my energy was being directed towards them instead, through a kind of manipulation, based on previous energy exchange in relation to them (that I guess), I was still holding on to, through my false constructed self. It's called (unfinished) business. The carrot used is: "What I thought I wanted from them is now being lavished upon me" as a Temptation, – thus I became Tempted, I was being led by a kind of trickery of the mind, the work of the custodian through another, but this time the pull isn't entire, because I manage to sustain most of myself to not succumb, this time realising that I no longer want them, or what they are offering in the way it is being offered, and never did. I just lacked boundaries, being that at the time I didn't value myself, however, I do now… and because I do now, I can now see that the temptation is a cloak for deception. - disguised as my perception of Love, because of the emotion that I had attached, and thus the energy invested. Love being all I've ever really wanted, but didn't know it, having never felt real love before, so was unable to recognise that what they were bringing wasn't it! Instead, they brought Just the issues I had surrounding it, the issues that attached me to the temptation thus being tempted (attracted).

My original investment with these past people was to enable my constructed self a place to hang and thrive, to play out our issues together in sheer blinded bliss! To remain fucked up and entwined in bullshit, like some sort of game, to ensure this book never sees the light of day, to guarantee I never see the light in 'My-Self'. With that said I quickly realise that it's a test of will, to see how much I want to remain on my path, and write this book, which is what I was put here to do! We will always be tested or assailed, just when we are about to break an illusion that covers our truth within the truth. The custodian will always send us a challenge through others to rock our foundation.

This is not an easy road to walk, but the only road to walk to free the 'Self.' You will let go of a lot of people and habits, not forcefully! but naturally. Emotions, if you choose to deal with something emotionally, it will create attachments, hence, further emotional investment is certain to leave a residue of 'self' behind, that will no doubt pull you back in at a later stage. The separation has to be done naturally to assure you no longer resonate with the person, situation or vibration, this will allow you to discover how they held you back, more importantly, how 'You' held Your-Self back. How by being entangled through energy exchanges, and colluding with outdated life story's and hidden wants, - you became trapped.

By identifying with perceived pain, and issues that none of you became responsible for, plugged you back into the illusion. How relating to them, and their trials not understood, awoke the trials you thought you had already dealt with, or didn't know you had, consequently threatening to pull you back in. You then realise that every time you overcome a fear or issue, it makes you stronger thus more resilient to the next test of intrusion that comes to prevent you from walking towards your freedom. People will try to draw you in by projecting their ideals and behaviours onto you, ideals and behaviours that mirror yours on an unconscious level but are unaware of. Remember! No one can hook you into a game or situation unless you already believe it to be your truth, your issue somewhere along the line. Hidden issues that used to trigger you into reacting in a way that would leave you drained, stuck, and confused will secure you a place in the fantasy land of projections (The Matrix), stuck in that particular issue accompanied by self-depreciation.

In order to see the reflection being shown to you, the mirror, the part of you that you can't see, the part of you that leads you into victim mentality mode - You have to be willing to let go of reacting to reactive triggers, and trust that you are safe. Do not associate with the emotion, Do not relate! choose to change your mind, to handle it differently. By ignoring the triggered emotion (Not reacting to it), you are choosing to relinquish control of losing control. By resisting the temporary boost you receive, gotten by syphoning the energy of the person who would be on your receiving end, choose to bear the emotion, feel it, as opposed to passing it on to another! Feeling the emotion is different to associating with it!

Allowing yourself to be triggered, by situations that your perception recognises as emotionally dangerous. Situations that bring up feelings, likened to those that have continually blocked you from a sense of happiness, or provoked anger, fear and debilitation in you, 'Will' prevent you from seeing through the veil of illusion.

The traumas of our past, grow many legs in order to keep us trapped by the original feeling, the original feeling is the attachment that keeps us on the mouse wheel in order to run the same dialogues (mental programming). This secures us to the 'Matrix', the constructed dimension we exist on, that prevents us from ever knowing ourselves. The part of us that is True Love, resides within, when sought and found, we 'Free The Self'. You must learn to transmute energy by flowing with it rather than against it, no matter how uncomfortable you first feel. When you become responsible for your own projections instead of transferring them to someone else, you will become aware that they are a construct, a false self. Reversed psychology becomes natural to you, - as you begin to understand the role you played in colluding. People will no longer be able to syphon your energy unless you let them! You will no longer give up your life force, through being made to feel the impact of sneaky unconscious emotions. You will no longer be led into ownership, or responsibility of the projection being presented by another, because it will no longer be part of you. You will no longer relate to it, the trigger will no longer have control over you, because you are no longer reactive to it. You then get to see who is asleep, clouded by their own judgements, criticisms, doctrines and issues.

When you are able to see this in operation, – when you can see what you used to do, or be like, in another, is when you have healed that particular issue within yourself. You will have also taken another step off the merry go round of illusions.

A person is unable to see you, if they can't see themselves! An example of this is: the counsellor who unconsciously avoids asking much needed questions pertaining to the client's growth, because they threaten to uncover their own unconscious issues. On the other hand, some counsellor's ask clients questions in order to make sense of their own neurosis. It is impossible for a counsellor to counsel if they themselves are not aware of self! In fact, all people who are not aware of self, will continue to always energetically pull you towards believing that you are a construct, a false self. It is necessary to be aware of self, sensitive to your environment, on both the spiritual realm and physical plane. You must pay attention to detail, be mindful that a projection can present itself in many forms, dependent on your objects of desire, wants and perceived needs.

Pay Attention! or You will become Lured, thus Assailed!

When you project onto someone else, you are trusting in their intuition and opinion, over that of your own. Result being; your very essence is left open to attack, each time destabilising you, leaving you in confusion, thus evidently compromising you, and placing you back into uncertainty, when otherwise you may have been clear. To be dependent on another for acceptance, will always lead you to fear of abandonment, and rejection (attachments). Relying on another's opinion, for decisions we should be making for ourselves, leaves us open to being judged by their standards and a victim of their hidden agendas, especially if they have bad intentions towards you, this may end up proving costly and dangerous to you in the long or short term! The real truth of the matter, is for you to remain conscious! Observe your projections instead of becoming them. Projections show your vulnerability, choose to understand that they have come from outside of you. However strange this may sound, the feeling of abandonment is actually your own protection - it is your own inherited ability, come to alert you to the fact that you have in-fact abandoned 'Your Self!'

# Principle {6}

Sex will either elevate you or undervalue and drain you. You need to know that it is not just a physical exchange of pleasurable fun.

Sex is sacred, it connects you telepathically, we are actually being vibrationally vulnerable with each other, allowing our souls to become connected! 'Sex' is not an act to be taken for granted, as if it's some sort of casual sport! You are actually bonding yourself to the person. When done through Love, it can be used to harness energy into creative power to manifest your good. When you have loving sex, you are harmonising, putting yourself into a place of trust with the person you are doing it with, thus generating positive energy. With that said! Random encounters will eventually destroy you! 'whether done for fun, carnal desire or some sort of fucked up sport', if not through love, you will be violating and compromising 'Self!', giving your energy away and creating soul ties with each other by leaving parts of yourselves behind.

Depending on whom you choose to have sex with, a person's essence can be locked into lower energy vibrations. By being enmeshed with another, you will become like 'them', but not in a good way. The act will also become a need, a game of control for both - vibrationally in relation to your issues and desires, - thus, the entities you carry. Fearing what they fear, you will see yourself as they see themselves. Basically, their fears become your fears! And your 'Strengths', which is the reason for the attraction to you! become there's, and vice versa! Fears you didn't have before being with them, or fears you already overcame, become reawakened parts of yourself you thought you had healed. Beware of who you energy exchange with! As everything required to uphold spiritual stability can only be done through 'Love', not 'Lust'. Vampire films are similes for what humans do to each other, they drain each other's lifeforce! That is why we are often tired after having sex rather than energised, because it is an exchange of frustrations, and body use. Literally, the action is demonic if not done with 'Love'. If your physical eyesight extended to the spirit realm, you would see an entity attached to you - it is there to specifically experience erotica through you, in order to syphon your life force. It is operating through another dimension with your cooperation, through the unconscious bond you have with your shadow, to alleviate the intensity of your disowned desires, 'known as lust'. You are not aware of its presence but you will feel it's anxiousness like a need. On this earth plane, the entity attachment is called, a succubus for female energy, and incubus for male. Our need to feel the warmth of each other's energy is the carrot used. We then go about enticing with sex to keep the connection, relationship alive. In order to do this, we begin to view ourselves as sex objects 'an object for sex', - the way of the Succubus and Incubus!

Some of us get this behavior mixed up with love, because the intensity of the lust is so spellbinding. Don't be fooled, you are being set up for body use, the use of your body! When sex is all a person wants from you, you will eventually become repelled by them. If you continue to have sex with them, you will be drained in order to feed them. Many people stay in connections just to feel the warmth of another's energy, 'Not' because they really want to be there. In the old days, married women would be told to 'lie back, close your eyes, and think of England'… and let the feeding commence, I guess! Watching porn has the same effect, if not worse because it becomes an addiction to visuals, the perfect opportunity for the entity to syphon your energy through instant transference! With that said! You would be Maintaining a very lonely, solitary existence in order to feed the entity. Beware of the opportunity… Beware of the 'Opportunist' attached to You!

Love, isn't what you are feeling when you think you are in love, that's why the feeling doesn't last long. The attraction you have found is someone who matches with the intensity of an original trauma, or karmic bond that you experienced on a parallel dimension. It is energy manifest, that has followed you through every dimensional existence that you have occupied. It is really an historical attachment likened to unfinished business, amassed over many lifetimes. It will remain with you until the root of the connection is recognised realised and dissipated. Sex, when not done through and with genuine Love, but instead through Lust, becomes the fueling of an attachment. The attachment picked up will stay with you until your need to match the intensity of the bond you had with the original host has gone.

When you refuse to feed the intensity, the power it has over you will lessen until its source is finally empty. You will then be released. You will then discover that it was a trauma bond that had you trapped all along... Now let's get into this!

The first thing one encounters after the honeymoon period of a new relationship, is the identification of what is not love or loving, your blocks within. Information we never processed comes back up when we get into relationships and close connections, mostly pertaining to trust. We buried those emotions from our past for a reason, because they were too painful to look at. We thought that by ignoring them they would no longer exist, when in reality we simply hid them within, in a deep dark dungeon, believing they would never need to be looked at again. You cannot hide your baggage if you want to enter into a genuine love connection! It has to come out, it has to be looked at, felt and healed in order for you to feel the true essence of the new connection and grow. Holding on to projections is resistance, it is what makes the awakening process so painful. The Mirrors are shown through each other's issues, to give us an opportunity to work through them together, or identify them within ourselves in order to be relinquished and dissipated. That's the real reason for attracting the relationship in the first place, to 'Heal'. However, when things become intolerable, if we are lucky we will decide that the relationship is not compatible and get out! But, if we choose to stay we are doomed, subjected to a reduction of energy, we endure pain and the loss of self, both trapped by each other's projections. The result being - power struggles to regain a semblance of the energy we had. Whoever's convictions are the strongest through draining the other, gets to be the leading force within the relationship, no matter how fucked up they are.

The draining will be asserted in all manner of ways, but mainly through your unconscious fears. Through continuous threats of leaving - fear of abandonment is created or reawakened., undeserved responsibility of the other, disregard of feelings and the list goes on. Potential drainage will always be triggered by something attached to the persons past collection of hidden issues and beliefs, all pertaining to not knowing themselves as a result of not having done the required work on themselves to clear their hidden thoughts, beliefs and traumas. The one who is carrying the most negativity becomes the controller, – thus embarking on an unconscious game, of seeking to recuperate what had been taken from them to create their issues in the first place.

When we relate to another's energetic pull, it instantly puts us onto the same vibration. The 'Negativity' they hold, overtime will overpower you and diminish you. Instead see them as a lesson come to challenge your self-worth, be open to whatever it is they have come to teach, process it then 'Walk Away!' It is not your responsibility to change them, or allow yourself to become a battlefield in order to ease and carry their pains. A being that is Self-Aware – Aware of 'Self' does not bother to seek to change another, because they know it will not work.

Life gets tricky when we haven't done any introspection. We attract what we are with regards to what we do not see, or realise about ourselves. Externally, a physical manifestation of what we are holding onto internally, becomes manifest in the behaviour of another. Unbeknown to us, this is our shadow side. Our job is to recognise it for what it is, instead of fighting and judging it, as we would only be fighting an aspect of ourselves.

You are given opportunities to change the trajectory of your life, but on many occasions, you choose to stay stagnant, by giving into attachments that lurk inside your energy field. You react to situations that trigger and regress you, instead of staying in the present, you surrender to dominating thoughts, that allow the fear held within them to take your energy, and 'Being' over. We need to let go of our habit of feeding negative energies that rise from within, held onto from the times when we felt helpless, and attacked. Unknown to us at the time, it is 'Not' really our fear! It is the fear held within the constructed self, it is it's fear of being dismantled and shut down. By giving in to the trigger, we are allowing the negative dialog to take over our senses, thus, rendering ourselves incapable of seeing the situation for what it really is; an opportunity to free ourselves from that particular vibrational hold. Instead we are unconsciously choosing to continue being our own inhibiter. We must learn to relinquish the chaos that keeps us stuck in the Matrix.

I went through a stage where I saw my fears as weaknesses, so denied and hid them. To be honest I didn't know they were there until I questioned why my life was the way it was. I didn't know they were constructs that had been created specifically to block any progress, I just thought I was weak and susceptible. The very things I would build others up for not acknowledging within themselves, were the very things unacknowledged on a certain level within me, manifested outwardly in others. They were mirroring to me what I had buried deep inside, - my talents and gifts. I could see the gold within them, but not believe it in myself. Understand, this is why I had an attraction to them, our similarities became the magnet - under a disguise of wanting to help them.

What I couldn't acknowledge in myself I saw in them... I was in an illusion within the illusion! I understood them, and wouldn't let them believe in the negative opinion they had of themselves, whilst at the same time I believed in the negative opinion I had of myself.
I had an essential need and drive to help them believe in themselves because nobody had ever believed in me. I didn't know that I was giving them what I needed to give to myself! This was an unrealised association, or should I say unconscious association to them. Subconscious association is what ties us all together on many levels. Recognition, a comradery between each other with association to our constructed shit, our issues! which we all unconsciously have in common, it's what keeps the matrix fueled, 'repetition'.

Attachments that are not conducive, or that do not relate to who and what we really are, must be released in order for us to free ourselves and ascend the matrix. We get karma back through staying with people, and situations that we know are no good for us, - choosing instead, to see our lives through 'Fear'. Not wanting or believing we can do better, or not wanting to be on our own. Whatever reason we relay to ourselves for not letting go, karma is shown through how they treat us - as a result of us choosing to stay, over and over again, by not listening to ourselves. We need to set boundaries for our own health, both spiritual and physical, or we will stay stuck in a cycle of attraction and repetition. Not seeing or accepting you have worth and value, slows you down, it holds you back from manifesting your 'Good'. In other words, you knowing the truth of something, and choosing to do nothing about it to your own detriment, is what will get You separated from Self.

The experiences we have, although some not fun at the time, come to teach us how to value ourselves, by showing us how we are 'Not' Valuing ourselves! by allowing us to experience what we have attracted, all pertaining to the unconscious beliefs we have attached to relationships.

You can't just be giving yourself, or of yourself to just anything or anyone! no matter who they are or what the circumstance presents. We need to become discerning to protect ourselves and our energy.

There are consequences, karma - for doing good, and being good to the wrong people. Ultimately, it will be served in the undesirable response we receive back, - sometimes from the people closest to you, – including your own children! Not being given due diligence or shown that you are valued, in the face of your kindness, disconnects you from your vitality, renders you emotional and takes away your ability to think logically, putting you on a lower vibration ready to enter the attachment of the victim mode. The insecurities contained within the bad enmeshment, transfer to you, by opening up wounds or creating beliefs you didn't have. By cleverly instilling doubt in a place where there was confidence, this creates the need for approval. The same applies when a person is deceptively valuing you, and love bombing you as a way to attach themselves to you. This lowers your guard in order for them to feed off your 'Good' intentions. They need to first destabilise you, this is how transference of energy works, by creating an opening, a weakness. It is a way of grooming you to accept that little, or 'No' effort from them, is normal, and all you deserve, in exchange for your investing in them, or investing in a situation that is undeserving of your energy and time! -

Your Karma, being no returns, love or validation - becoming the things you think you now need from them. By turning themselves into a need, they can syphon energy from you, thus, giving them further control. Your efforts being met with a lack of appreciation, disregard and a sense of entitlement from the receiver, teamed with hostility, - over time will 'Destroy' you.
If you paid attention to the dynamics of previous relationships you would understand that you were being shown what to look out for and what to avoid, - Not what to fall for or embrace… 'The Trap!' It becomes a trap when you don't pay attention to what the person or situation is making you feel and leading you to believe. What are you thinking at the time? are there any red flags or any emotional remembrances that you are choosing to ignore? Are you driven into a battle of passivity with your opponent? Have you allowed them to groom you into keeping things as they are, through your own fear of letting go for whatever reason? Or do you choose to collude and cooperate in the romance of the love bomb or bad treatment instead? These kinds of situations and foundations are not built on anything real! They are built on deceiving yourself. You need to find strength and courage within, and have the determination to want to move forward. When the people you are attached to, don't show who they really are, they stunt your growth through you holding on to the notion of them, or the impression 'they' have sometimes given you of them! Not the truth of them! We cannot evolve or grow within a false foundation, or with someone who is faking who they are, – to at a later date reveal themselves when they think you have become sufficiently disarmed. They are inevitably putting an end, or delay to the spiritual aspect of themselves, and 'You', through association thus stunting your growth in one way or another.

We must continue to be mindful of where we put ourselves. Remember! Whatever is happening to us is deliberately manifested to lead us into knowing ourselves, 'Not' hold us back! As long as you want emotional reciprocation, validation or are seeking self-value from a person - you will become tied, you will unconsciously become submissive and emotionally controlled by that person's particular energy vibration, blinded into believing that one day they will give you the appreciation and respect you believe you deserve, all pertaining to the amount of emotional energy/investment you have put into them. However, the person knows that once given, it will free you from the attachment, thus stopping the continued flow of energy you provide them - in order to feed the entity they carry. Hence one of you is being fed, and the other is the food, thus being drained. Meaning, one has an entity, and the other colluding with it! You will find yourself arguing or rather, battling, to occupy your own space and place, in your own world, both spiritually and physically. Others will feed from your unawakenedness. As they syphon your energy you become the victim of the opportunist. We must learn to become discerning! in order to survive on this planet/physical plane we exist on. Nothing is real, it is all made up of deceptions that keep us in worship of the programmed constructed false-self! Emotions are outside of us, they reside in our energy field – aura, or rather our energy body just outside of our physical body, they hold us down to prevent our growth by severing our awareness to self. We must never depend on anyone or anything for acceptance.

We are here to learn to accept ourselves, in order to relinquish attachments. We have been fooled into becoming responsible for each other, by mere association to a story that reflects in likeness to ours. Be mindful, not everyone is a match, opposites do not attract in a healthy way, – one will always debilitate the other.

It is not easy to get out of a connection, situation-ship, because it temporarily provides you with relief in association to trauma, along with the other issues grown as a result. Instead of using the connection as your battleground to offload fears and attachments that you refuse to face, - choose to loosen such attachments, by dissipating the hook to the energy flow that feeds them. We do this by no longer associating with, or to them. When a thought goes around in your head, 'Let' it speak and you listen, do not interrupt or conversate with it - let it play out like a tape recorder, instead of trying to do affirmations over it, and giving it your attention. Leaving it with nothing to hook on to, it will then pass over you. You'll be amazed with what you hear. Express the emotions attached, then let go! Become discerning like the 'Observer'. 'Do Not Forget', it's your shadow, it is ok, be 'Brave' (just let it speak till it's had enough)! The attachment will then dissipate naturally, – replacing what was once a draining neurosis, with space that releases you from its lower vibrational hook and trigger. This is how we enable ourselves to store and harvest our own energy, – instead of having it syphoned from us through reacting to said thoughts, feelings or situation. When you stop associating with the attachment, – the thought, feeling or situation, the energy fueling it dissipates. When it dissipates, there will no longer be anything blocking you from Self, you then become the Observer, – then projections from others will no longer work.

# Principle {7}

It is true that man cannot worship two Gods, – one assures your death both physically and spiritually, the other gives you life. Unaware on many levels the majority seem to be embracing the god of death (materialism) due to the fact that they can physically see the perceived fruits of their labour, seeming to have an un-ruff-arable loyalty, being totally oblivious to what is and always has been at stake, or on a stake if I'm to be honest.

The God I am referring to is the Infinite Source of All Creation, Omnipotent Most High. This is 'Not' the same lord god worshiped in the bible or any other religious scriptures! Let's face it, that lord god or gods as its written in plural in the bible, further suggests there are many of them, - goes around killing magnitudes of people including babies, - loads of boys at one point!

Is jealous, discriminates, has a sexual preference, inflicts fear and starvation, seems to promote a hierarchy pertaining to skin colour and cast, is a (He) who sacrifices, and has many aliases who live amongst the pages of numerous religious doctrines, – the list goes on! What I am about to explain, and guess you haven't given any thought, is the word 'lord' in the bible - doesn't lord mean: a man of noble rank, or high office, a man who is revered in Parliament, - a man of means! I mean, God is God right, (one word) but, in the bible, (that is written by man), the title of lord has been strategically placed in front - which suggests that the lord god (in the bible) is none other than a man, imbued with the custodian entity. Who throughout the bible wishes to be regarded as a god! This is trickery, wordplay, used as part of the 'Programming' played on you, deliberately done, and by 'No' mistake I might add! People are really worshipping a set of humans. Through affirmation, blindness and blinkers, your senses are in captivity to an entity of greed and desire, that you will never be permitted to satisfy. Represented by lords', people of means, and Noblemen! to keep you in the mindset of fodder! Of no importance, destined to forever look upon the ones with wealth, as being better than you! The lord, ultimately to be feared and shit scared of offending forever. – know your place... Amen! Amen, said to mean 'Let it be so', or 'So be it!' actually derives from the name Amun Ra, – another play on words, a spell even? please investigate this for yourselves. However, let's just say, the word broken up says, 'A men' - a man!

You have been manipulated and blinded through the pages of the bible, to believe the lord is the infinite 'Creator of All', when it is far from the truth, – actually, to say far is an understatement, it needs to say 'Eternally!' The lord god in the bible has nothing to do with God the infinite Creator of All. Consider elitism, wealth and the obtaining of it, (which is what these lords stand for) The bible is speaking of a man or rather Men! who is in a position of authority, who calls himself lord, or who is called lord by those who are subservient to him, or are of lower inferior position to him! The worship of human Kings and Queens, is a big deal here on planet earth, ever wondered why? If you pick up the King James version of the bible dated 1611, you will see that no reference is made to the word lord, – it was just God, from genesis chapter (1) verse (1) up to verse (31) the bible only speaks of God, - it isn't until chapter (2) that the word lord in capital letters appears! Please Consider what I am saying to you here! Anyway, without going into it further, I advise you to do some investigating, look up what lord means for yourself, then consider why it has been placed in front of the word god, and given to be digested as a truth to every country to worship and affirm, as there only reference to reality... Why? Remember, what I said earlier about the media, and the narrative those in influential positions would have us believe, in order to retain their positions? Yes! The bible's (lord god) of the plane we exist on, shares a seat with the custodian who peddles materialism and wealth, as the ultimate substitute for self-worth! If obtained it is the only way to garner respect, but only as long as it is obtained with a mindset pertaining to its own... the custodian!

The custodian and lord god don't actually have their own energy, it needs to use ours to exist. The biggest deception is the constructed belief that material wealth equals and amounts to Self-Worth! Thus, in order to earn the right to feel valued, worthy, powerful or have some semblance of power, and be respected by others on this planet; your physical attributes, along with how much money and things you have amassed, must become of paramount importance. These are all human perceived facets and ideals, programmed into you that became part of your belief system. Your amount of monetary wealth here is a belief you have adopted to determine the totality of your worth! However, it is an untruth, an attachment, a trick, and distraction of the custodian, because the real true currency is your 'Energy Life Force!' You constantly 'Give it Away' by paying attention – or rather 'paying with your Attention!' Attention equals Energy!

The custodian and the infinite Creator of All, are of the same energy, just at opposite polarities! In the sense that the custodian is not separate, just devoid, – the voice outside of the self, projecting negative thought forms into your awareness, that when listened to become your reality and part of your belief system. Its job is to direct you away from your essence, energy life force, the infinite Creator of All, You, your creator within, - your spirit. However, because you have been imbued with infinite creative energy, albeit hidden, you will always be unconsciously pulled towards home! Because you do not truly belong here.

That is why you have had no choice but to come back over and over again, to be awakened a little more each time until you remember. How long this takes, is up to you, that is, if you choose to pay attention.

I named this book 'Two Fuckers Playing Chess using Us as Pawns' because, our soul, life force and the necessity to hold on to it is what we are here to realise, however, this is a game of two conflicting energies, We belong to neither through free will, but originate from 'One', - difference between the two, - is 'One' is Love, home, void of pain in all forms, structure and stature, non-physical in nature and essence, liquid/fluid, as in, it is part of 'Everything', Whereas, the other creates pain, feasts on fear and lust, bases self-worth on materialism, – then syphons the energy of the neurosis it creates in us, through all of the above - to feed it. One is the Infinite Creator of All, and the other is the devil custodian entity. My ego is a narcissist, pertains to the ego being the construct, the false programmed self, and agent for the custodian. It encourages us to go in directions that ultimately bring pain and disappointments, with empty promises, rejection and hurt. After you have fulfilled the said ego action/desire, you experience that following it's direction amounts to nothing, likened to a trick, a false guidance!

You are then filled with punishing passive or aggressive negative thought forms, and left empty for having followed it in the first place! Burying you deeper into a level of self-denial. Denial that you are a life force independent of exterior wants, denying that you exist, and thus driving you to trust in what is seen with physical eyes to be your point and sense of reality. Along with emotions, sensations and the need for physical touch, this is all accepted through our unconscious need to belong.

# Principle {8}

The custodian enlists entities that attach themselves to people, who then subsequently come after you (through attraction to your Attachments) in order to block you from becoming aware of your true self. Confusion will then tie you up in knots and render you senseless, (de-sensitise you) – the entity attaches to past trauma and situations that had emotionally affected you. All making it impossible for you to decipher between what has been triggered by your past, and what is currently playing out in your life, albeit through different people and situations.

We are being prevented from relating our past to what we experience in our present. We are being Prevented from understanding the importance of the correlation they have, with regards to us not growing spiritually or mentally, we are stuck in a damaged unfulfilled child mode, the 'Shadow'.

The unacknowledged unconscious emotions and thoughts are being continuously pulled up to be healed, but instead of realising this, we reject and ignore them to be so, so instead they circle around as words, negative perceptions, projecting onto others through our dialogue, as false truths and deceptions, which in turn haunt our personalities, by presenting ourselves as prey to those who feed, – we become gullible, thus keeping ourselves in a cycle of repetition and shadow. 'False ego worship', looking outside of ourselves for validation, approval, and help. When our efforts are not reciprocated we become blocked. This drains our life force and weakens the connection we have with the infinite creative energy of Love, 'Our Selves'.

Once we forget that we are loved by the infinite Creator of All, we seek refuge in people, and by obtaining things as a temporary substitute for a sense of self-worth. Over time we realise that we will never obtain enough to sustain our wants, so we begin to drain each other, by means of attachment and attention seeking. This is our way of getting approval, 'Through the game', a game of manipulation, learnt behaviours developed during childhood through control dramas, (anyone read the Celestine Prophecy?). All dramas derive from a need to get something not provided, or developed within during our early years, at the time we are most impressionable. Humanity lacks humility and integrity as a result!

The scapegoat, and black sheep of the family will know only too well what it is like to be drained, and used as the family dustbin, for others to put their rubbish into, - metaphorically speaking.

I explained earlier in the book, how we attract relationships in order to heal what we haven't dealt with pertaining to buried issues. Those issues originally came from childhood, later to become entrenched in adulthood, brick by brick as part of the personality. However, I'm not about to go into the psychology of nurture, I am banking on you already knowing that, plus this book isn't about the fucked-up people we encountered growing up, it's also not about feeling sorry for ourselves, or hating the fuckers, it's about seeing, and acknowledging the jewels in the treatment we received. Your being attracted to this book is no coincidence; it's because you want to know how to get home, what you are, and where you really come from, - how to relinquish your pain, and reap the positivity within it, how repetition really works, how you are still being controlled, and how, when you set out to do a thing differently, you get the same non-productive results. You want to be 'Free'. So, let's continue!

It is true that everything holds energy, like when you walk into a room, you can tell if there has been tension, not just by the expressions on people's faces, but by the energy, vibe, you feel coming from them, and the environment you have entered; that is if you are empathic enough to feel and sense it? However, if you are not, you will experience the environment with camaraderie, as in, all false egos teaming up with focused resentment towards the one who shines the brightest, and in awe of the one showing most confidence likened to arrogance in the room.

We can feel another's energy; we can also hear what they are thinking in our energy field, unknowing that we are capable of receiving, or even receive these communications. They come as preparation for us to construct an answer, or response if any demands are forthcoming that we do, and do not wish to entertain, either mentally or physically. At the moment the awareness of this gift is blocked from you, however, once you realise that you are empathic - sensitive, you will know that you already knew this! However, your blocks, (false self) will not permit you to be aware, so, instead you continue to believe it is you, thinking and feeling, thus react in accordance to your already constructed beliefs. As an example: I recall the countless times I've been in a happy vibe/mood, then encountered someone who says they are ok, for me to then, be pulled almost magnetically, into becoming overcome by heavy feelings and emotions of wanting to cry, minutes into connecting with the conversation! Then, as soon as I realise that the magnetic pull, and emotions are not mine, the now intrusive energy leaves my aura/body, and the person begins to express the truth of how they are really feeling. If my realisation does not occur, my energy field will remain like a buffer for them to transfer their emotions and gain extra energy to sustain the projection, as I would be quietly accepting the handover, and support what is hidden within them from them. By me sending it back, they are unable to deny the emotion that belongs to them, they are also unable to contaminate me by leaving me with it when they walk away.

However, God forbid if you have anything hidden within your shadow that remotely matches their emotion! It is true what they say about misery liking company, misery attracting misery, because if the same emotion matches with you, (an emotion you may be hiding within your shadow) it will seek you out to assure its own longevity. You will find yourselves swapping vibrational notes, this is in relation to all human emotion! A good example is of a conversation between myself and someone years ago: She was commenting on how skinny she thought I was, saying I needed to put weight on, I had no issues with my body, so instead of buying in to it and agreeing with her, I consciously paid attention. I noticed that she was in fact overweight so I chose to just smile, keep my mouth shut and wait. Then honestly, in the next breath she began to say that she needed to go on a diet and exercise more and that she wasn't happy with 'Her' weight... Bingo! Me choosing not to relate played out with her owning what was her truth 'Not Mine!' All transference is done unconsciously, I don't even think she was aware of what she just tried to do to me, she probably just knew that it would make her temporarily feel good, 'By trying to make me feel bad!' With me not choosing to own her shit by agreeing with her that I needed to put weight on she had no option but to own it! If I had I would've gone home believing I had body issues. Also, if I already believed that I was too skinny, or even gone into sympathy with her, our conversation would've been a match and I guess lasted a lot longer! As we would've both wallowed in a narrative of body depreciation, however, the double ended sword would've been, if she was successful at making me feel inadequate, by agreeing with her instead of pushing her energy back to her.

Next time I would've been the overweight one and she the slim one… because I would've unwittingly exchanged my energy vibration for hers! That is how the custodian works (through people) this is how the custodian keeps us asleep and docile, through energetically relating to each other's neurosis. Never healing or coming to any conclusion within, on a cycle repeating the same bullshit over and over again, slinging the same kind of mud in the same pit together, led by physical needs, wants, desires, inadequacies, and jealousies, judgements pertaining to the so called 7 deadly sins. Which were originally manifest from Proverbs in the, (Yes, You've Got It) the bible! It's so fucking twisted but clever at the same time. It's not just mainstream media, or the people we have accepted as guardians to wield power over us, so-called 'royalty', manipulating us with shameless standards of living that we could never adhere to, 'Lording' over us with disgusting displays of opulence, that through taxes we are paying for! In other words, we are giving them 'free' money, our money to live a high life, to live in splendor at our expense, for us to look 'up' to them, like they are some sort of reward! all because we have been programmed to perceive them as higher, and better than us, worthier than us. Encouraging a belief that we, the people are merely subjects, when really, we are all the same! In fact, their family dynamics are more toxic than most! In all honesty, what the fuck do they do for the people? Some would say; "but they bring money into the economy"… (how?) because the people never see any of it! Also, as the people, in general, we are not given any choice as to where our money goes or what it is spent on!

The majority are struggling to survive, to eat, to even have a basic standard of living, which should be our inherent right! All we see is them parading and prancing about on red carpets wearing bloody crowns, that no doubt someone died to mine the jewels for. Some will say, its tradition, whose tradition? what fucking tradition? Where did it come from? Who said that people are to look up to them, and be in sacrifice through taxes for them? Which all translates down to, the syphoning of 'Our Energy'. I will not highlight the so-called abolishment of human slavery, because it is still rife in some places, and cloaked in others. What I will highlight however, is that we are all slaves, even those who are materially rich! They are slaves to their wealth! and state of mind! Thus, 'The Custodian!' who likes to be continuously paid! Nobody is better than anybody! therefore, nobody is better off than anybody really, and if truth be known, it is all an illusion, another distraction, – Kings and Queens in this day and age... delusions of grandeur! what the fuck? You need to wake up people!

In one way or another, although on a smaller scale, but all the more relevant, with regards to surplus to requirement, - people are doing the same manipulations to each other, one way is by desiring to keep up with the Jones's or Kardashians! - nowadays... Not forgetting that even if we give sympathy to a person who is neurotic we are fucked!

The custodian has no energy of its own, it has to get humans to believe in it to fuel it, and what better way to do this, than through our perceived inadequacies, that have been constructed for us to think, then believe to be our own. Remember, we are spirit housed in a physical body existing on a physical plane, – everything that comes into us comes from outside of us. The job of the custodian is to separate us from our consciousness, – we are not aware of this, because we do not know our consciousness exists! The Self is hidden; therefore, we have no awareness of a self, the custodian uses our vulnerabilities against us.

# Principle {9}

My process has been painstaking and arduous, entirely necessary and of paramount importance! Above all, to experience and decipher it, is my entire reason for being here. In order to protect the truth of what I am, I've had to learn how to hold on to my energy and prevent it from being taken, drained, and harvested by the custodian. The custodian entity uses our energy to fuel the control it has over the essence of the masses, - the multiple spirits housed in physical bodies on this planet. I had to learn this, in order to combat the attacks that tried to weaken me by syphoning my life force. Programming that is constructed to prevent me from manifesting my sense of worth, thus blocking me from becoming aware of my true origin.

Our memories have been wiped, almost all recollection of who and what we are is hidden from us. We are named 'humans' although we are spirit, - consciousness, sometimes called the soul, housed in a physical body. - We are living an inferior existence under the indoctrination of the custodian entity. Our spirit has taken on the physical appearance of the body, the denseness of that body created an ego as its counterpart, a constructed self, 'Personality' that adheres and recognises everything physical. We the people are in denial of the spiritual, our soul, our conscious, – our inner world, other planes and dimensions of existence that run parallel to this earth plane, that our life force simultaneously occupies. Unknown to us we are multidimensional beings.

When I was younger and at school - I can honestly say that I pretended I was stupid, (not a word I would normally use because its negative), however, it is the only word that comes to mind, meaning, - in my case, that I didn't have the mental capacity to work things out with regards to academia, in relation to this world. It's not even that I didn't have the capability, because I did! It's that I didn't have enough interest in order to access it, although I knew it was there. Basically, I knew I wasn't bloody stupid, but didn't know how to decipher that I wasn't. So, because nothing was forthcoming inside me, which pertained to what is perceived as the knowledge of this world, 'nothing' was reflected back as being of any relevance. As a result, I had 'nothing' within that related me to what I was being taught to prove the (stupid label) any different. So! In that sense it was an early distraction, because I believed it, although unconsciously, I already knew that earth-so-called- knowledge, and 'Knowledge' were two different things.

However, as my memory of who and what I really was, had been hidden, there was nothing to cushion me from believing it, therefore, it became a false truth within me, and the beginning of a complex, an (Attachment), I guess, (as she writes a Book). I also had the kind of teachers around me that only seemed to give attention to the ones that were easy to teach, the ones that fed on academic information. The children like me were relegated to what can only be described as the 'thicko' class, to get extra tuition, in an attempt to get us to conform and receive help with the subjects that we struggled to understand. Although no real work was ever done or completed, due to the teachers always being supply teachers with no real quality of interest from them towards us, and us! Well, not Me! Although I would laugh, - The students being frustrated, would become confrontational, thus providing entertainment and distraction, due to feeling inadequate in comparison to the children who understood, and were seen to be thriving! Although if you were to give any of us a creative task, we would absolutely top marks it! Back in normal class, History lessons felt like false information and one up man ship. Like there were bits missing, with only one race being given the credit for absolutely everything. Along with 'the' other stuff, it was also information that I just didn't resonate with. As a child I was made to feel ashamed, Especially as black people were always first shown to us as people with bones through their noses, ripped up cloth or a string of leaves around their waists, with breasts hanging out carrying bloody spears - which the white kids would snigger at in the back of the class.

you can imagine the racist ones would be loving it, which was fine because they'd get a slap at the end of lesson (JOKING!) I don't condone violence! However, sometimes it is the only result... although it is never the answer. Just to add, all indigenous 'Tribes People' around the world, of every colour and creed, despite losing most of your homeland along with the riches it contains, some of you not even permitted to enjoy your own beach land, or plough the land that is inherently yours! You, having held on to 'Your' authenticity and spiritual ideals, is something that deserves the upmost respect, and should be treasured and valued by us all! Instead, your precious minerals, sustenance, ancestral wisdom and creations have been taken, and distributed around the world to profit others! all except You! leaving you with nothing to barter with or sustain yourselves. Many of you made to become silenced with toxic handouts (Africa, Australia), specifically served to take you down and render you incoherent, or worse! is an absolute travesty and pure savagery!
I won't even mention the absolute desecration of Haiti.

## May You All, One Day Find Your Way Home x

I just never really wanted to know what they were teaching in school because it simply did not feel like the truth, being made to pay attention to shit that I had absolutely no interest in, that was not going to benefit me as an adult. It was a place that I felt we were forced to go to, in hindsight to be indoctrinated, and initiated into the matrix programmed cult, the way to assure that we are further separated - from The Self! to remain believing we were the fodder of society, – likened to what they do in the army, strip you of who you are, to then rebuild you into something subservient that is going to be productive to them.

With regards to the army, a physical 'empty' killing machine! - upon retirement most left drained - feeling odd amongst society, not supported, in spite of giving their lives to fight in battles they had 'No' business fighting, some left haunted by PTSD. With regards to us, a docile obedient machine! washed of all individuality and self-awareness. School… I always felt that I was too old to be there, and at times knew more than the teacher, with regards to problem solving and social maturity, as most teachers were just on a power trip. The draining of a child's energy is rife in our schools. I thought that as long as I learnt the basics, I would be sort of 'ok' out in the world. I can safely say that I learnt more when I had left! – I also realise that I never did need to learn algebra amongst other things! So, it makes sense that I didn't! Or rather, Couldn't. So, with the school system, along with emotionally unavailable, narcissistic parenting, the traumas that I experienced at the hands of the deprived are too many to mention, but hit across the board of what you would expect from people with no morals, and a lack of integrity, energy vampires who don't give a shit about self-awareness or themselves, let alone a child in their care.

As an adult, I too ended up becoming marginally brainwashed into what is coined today as a people pleaser and over-giver, with a victim mentality. I over compensated for the imposed beliefs given to me by those who parented me, - that I was inadequate, wasn't wanted, not good enough or deserving, was of 'No' value, 'Never' validated, so went about seeking the love and approval of others, through words and deeds, to my own detriment, - with regards to what I had left of my energy life force. I believed in what people said, rather than take note of their actions, - what they did. An example of this would be: a person would lull me into a sense of friendship, elicit my trust, then over a short space of time, stab me in the back (not literally). The friendship, the word used, being a lie, would seem to hurt me more than the physical action of the stabbing, although metaphorical, it became literal because it is deception (being deceived). To protect myself from eliciting such treatment, I had to understand where it was coming from and how I was attracting it. In order to shield myself against false friends, and relationships (custodian vibration), I had to understand that the pain of the stabbing was in fact worse, and learn to value myself. Confused? Because unconsciously, it is what I believed I deserved, – so was unconsciously compliant in seeking it. Ok, so if you think about it, the stabbing is what I was unknowingly aiming for, because it would confirm what I was already made to believe I deserved. I was taught to trust people at face value, not by their deeds, 'Not' by my intuition, as I wasn't permitted to trust in that as a child either, hence why I became blind to it. Result being - Trusting in others instead of myself, rendered me incapable of becoming aware of when they were going to let me down, hurt me or deceive me.

It was like I was shut off to the signs, so instead I would become devastated, then numb, and left thinking that 'I' must have done something wrong, consumed by 'guilt', all being the 'Pay off'. All this being familiar with the dynamics of the parenting I received, and the people I grew up around, – I was groomed to view bad treatment as sort of endearing, in a fucked-up kind of way. A slap from an abusive boyfriend meant he cared about me, or he wouldn't have bothered to do it, – how 'absolutely' fucked is that! Truth being, I was carrying hidden attachments, that stemed from particular males in my family, who got a rise out of expressing that kind of behavior, as if it were some kind of sport to be exerted upon me. All 'Cleverly' designed to further confirm and entrench what I believed the truth about myself to be, in order to assure I go back and have it happen to me all over again, albeit with different people having the same character as the ones before. You would think I would've learnt from the previous amount of pain to not step back? However, I didn't because it wasn't that cut and dry, – I was actually powerless to prevent repetition happening. It's like my mind, my constructed self would always lead me into the hands of a situation, or somebody unscrupulous, who would try to take advantage of me, believing that they had an entitlement to my energy my attention, and 'Me'. Conditioned to believe I should give it. I do not blame them as it was part of a control drama, rooted from what I believed needed to be validated within me! We all unconsciously work together to confirm our beliefs, (me believing in a lack of self-worth) which translates into a need to be accepted, loved and belong, whilst at the same time, believing I, – we, don't deserve it.

I was doubly confused So, would dangerously, 'unconsciously' attract suitable candidates to assist me in confirming this as my truth, in order to keep the cycle going. – It was the hit of the let-down, a feeling of guilt that I hadn't done enough, the (bad treatment) that I was familiar with and attached to. Until one day I couldn't take any more, my mind was frying! It actually hurt to focus on an ant crawling on the ground. Without going into too much detail, – the 'Opening'. A friend had come to see me, worried! She deliberately called me all manner of names to get a reaction, result being I didn't bat an eyelid… I just said my mind hurts, with that said - she became concerned and left, to promptly return with a book and gave it to me. Within 24 hours I had read it, I couldn't put it down, well, only to go for a toilet break and a snack, but only because my stomach began to rumble so loud that I couldn't ignore it, otherwise I would've. I had never really been interested in reading books, the closest I had ever come to a book is the 7-foot tower of cosmopolitan fashion magazines, which I had collected over the years, which sat piled upon each other in the corner of my front room. When I started to read this book it resonated with me, with my being, the author talked about things and situations she had experienced, likened to what I was going through, and mildly explained how I was giving my power away! It was a remarkable book, given to me at the exact right time. It opened me up, which gave me an opportunity to see. I was then able to understand and destabilise my compacted hidden layers of untruth, I was able to awaken to a 'Sense of Self' as being real.

It uncovered what I needed to validate in myself, in order to save and preserve what was left of 'Me', or rather, of 'My' energy left within me. I realised that I wasn't being authentic, or honest, I had been misleading myself. From then on, I was fully committed to waking up and reclaiming all the splintered parts of myself, - energy that was taken from me. I also felt committed to helping others to grow, by sharing the information I was learning. Like I said earlier, the journey isn't easy, however, the challenges are all necessary once you accept the path.

Eventually being authentic became more important than pleasing people. I realised that my energy was being used by others to fuel their constructed false selves. I began to notice that they would energetically attack me, pulling on me, either passively or aggressively, whenever I remotely came across as if I was going to say 'No', or if I had worked out that they were just using me. When I'd pull back my energy of attention, - I wouldn't hear from them, or they would become cold and condescending (projecting onto me), then, my constructed self would kick-in, leaving me feeling as if I had done something wrong, and guilty for thinking that 'they' had. Clever, they would do this I guess to cover up the fact that they were the ones who had been disingenuous to me. Previous to my realisation, I would've been blind to it, and through guilt endeavored to do more for them. False friendships or relationships that were noticeably one-sided, with effort and investment of energy all coming from me! with people who seemed to think my role was to specifically serve them, became empty when I decided not to conform with the role of the fodder, (a person of little importance), At that point they would side-eye me.

As they could no longer use me, instead they became competitive towards me, which would dampen my self-esteem by saddening me. This retort from them always surprised me, because I had never felt any form of rivalry towards them, or shown any, - if anything, I played myself down. Truth is, they were never really my friends, it was 'just me' who thought they were. The dynamics of my family, along with the role given to me showed up in every relationship. Unconscious to me, at the time, allowing them, was my only way to feel what I thought was love, and regard.

Consciously I wanted the people around me to grow, become independent, self-aware and self-reliant, but instead they became reliant on my attention, and saw me as food, a meal that they were entitled to eat, because I was readily accessible and always keen to help, I seemed to always be there for them. As a result, I was easily taken for granted. This was draining me, leaving me with nothing to direct or manifest my life with. They were using what I had shared, (my energy) to build themselves up, then come back for a top up when they felt energetically low. Instead of understanding what was being given, and using it as a start to generate the energy for themselves, they chose to whittle it away through a lack of courage when challenged. This 'lack' would always result in them becoming spiritually greedy, I must say that, being infused with a boost of energy can at times become addictive to some. Meanwhile, at the same time my desire to be helpful was a trick, a self-deception!

You see, through my lack of understanding, with regards to how energy works, by continuously giving of myself, by relating to people (obviously in order to help them) I tricked myself into being in sacrifice to others, 'The Martyr', and creating soul tie's, attachments, and ending up drained with nothing left to sustain myself. I later realised that on an unconscious level, my desire to be so helpful to my own detriment, was really about abandonment issues stemming from when I was a child. Somewhere inside I had confused my story with theirs, so sought to create a corrective environment for them, because I didn't have one. I listened to them whereas no one else had, in a hope of preventing them from having to feel pain like I did. I helped them whereas no one else would. Instead they took the bloody piss, choosing to wallow in my energy instead, I then had to learn how to become discerning, learn to say 'No', without feeling that I was wronging them.

To be objective and perceptive no matter what situation you find yourself in, be it perceived Love, soul mate, twin flame, friends, volunteer doormat, over giver! Or 'Workhorse' - in the collective energy of society related.

It is Within the Letting Go, that You Regain Your Flow.

Most ties are maintained through a false unconscious belief - that one has a responsibility to another, under the disguise of being understanding as in unconditional, (no conditions placed), including the acceptance of another's wrongful treatment towards you, therefore you rationalise it. Whilst at the same time if you are harbouring a sense of inadequacy, hidden fear or rejection and abandonment issues, you are unknowingly strengthening and feeding 'the constructed self'. The constructed self/Ego, feeds off the hidden shadows that lurk in the subconscious, the ones we are not aware of having created any damage. You would've known they are there because discomfort will arise when antagonism gets close, however, over time the discomfort feels like comfort, and a signal of correct action - thus normal to you... yes, that's how messy you are. These actions or rather, 'programmed responsibilities' secure a flow of energy out. This catering, is the need of the giver who gets to remain useful, (a pleasure to the people pleaser) and thus un-abandoned, whilst remaining enslaved to the greedy appetite of the receiver, who has secured themselves a steady flow of power, likened to an invisible contract, serving to assure both parties stay hooked to each other, thus hooked up to the Matrix to continue a cycle of repeat actions and situations! No matter who you do it with, the behaviour is secured, as long as the catering continues, neither will ever experience growth, (blinded by the illusion of the master slave mentality) which of course, is the Master Custodian Programme, 'The Matrix'.

Attachments picked up from others, dictate what you experience, because they end up becoming 'your' beliefs, – unknowingly carrying another's issues in your energy field and believing it is yours, is the way of the empath. A way to explain this would be; for no apparent reason, having an undercurrent fear of expressing something, that you know you are good at, accompanied by obsolete unrelatable words appearing to come from your mind, telling you that you can't do it, and not to bother. These thoughts cancel out the good energy you had, by invading your energy life force. Although these thoughts don't belong to you, they will literally debilitate you and hold you back, preventing you from moving forwards, whilst at the same time creating a fear of success, – and notions that don't even belong to you! Trauma creates holes that others can attach themselves to. As long as you accept that the energy of the issue is yours, – through relating to it, they, the person offloading it, in turn will receive your good, your confidence, and undoubtably what was meant for you. Guilt and lack of self-worth, relating to people with unfortunate stories, amplifies yours, and cushions theirs, leaving you to feel emotions and issues that were otherwise theirs! Thus, – Empathy is a double ended sword if you do not know how it works.

# Principle {10}

Speaking what one observes, rather than storing it up inside, 'Is' self-validation! Wanting for nothing outside of the self, - whilst remaining open to everything, equals not holding back. This means, one is aware they already have everything within; thus, having self-acceptance and approval - 'Your, own acceptance and approval!'

    The family... I decided to speak my truth, and tell them what I thought of them. As I spoke, my heart and chest felt like they were going to beat out of my body. For the first time, I didn't give a fuck about offending their feelings, nothing! I didn't give a fuck about being perceived as the bad one either, if truth be known, they had always treated me as if I were some sort of leper, the outsider! They would have get togethers and leave me out. That's when they weren't playing favorites.

On occasion I had been called the runt of the family by my uncle, mothers favourite name for me was - the cunt! I was treated accordingly. Obviously, they were projecting onto me how they felt about themselves. I had nothing to lose, so gave back, and let out what they had been preventing me from expressing, due to believing them. Release the things that would surely end it, all in relation to them, but in my own defense. 'My' truth, the truth! The things that were used to tie me to them, keep me trapped, in a web of my own deceit, created by them. I became deceived through my own inability to tell my truth, through fear of losing them, because somewhere inside me I believed 'they' were all I had. Conditioning had taught me that I must try and convince them that I am good, and worthy, by accepting the position I had been given in order to receive their love. I also believed I was already alone. So, I no longer cared what the consequences were, I didn't care enough about them anymore for it to hurt, I just wanted to be 'Free'. Through them, the custodian had placed within me unconscious consequences, meaning, always being on edge. One day they would laugh at something I said, then the next day they would want to knock me out for it, - they were able to not only plant fear of having an opinion into me, but also use their knowledge of my hidden fear of rejection and abandonment against me…, basically, they knew which buttons to press. They used the 'Love' I had for them to control me! Constantly triggering me, thus reminding me on a certain level that I must be grateful, must be quiet, - believe and treasure what they had compounded upon me!

However, through me no longer giving a fuck, I was able to adjust the power they had over me, I had realised that no matter how much of myself I gave over to them, it was never going to be enough. It was like a pressure release along with anger, it's like guilt had been hidden inside me, covered by fear, and a responsibility to be understanding, withholding, and loyal, keep secrets and allow them to fester and kill me. Releasing all of that shit felt like my vibration was going to come out of my mouth, I could feel it all over my body, it was so strong, it felt like something was coming off me, being literally taken off me! Like a spell that had been cast, had now been removed... broken. It didn't matter to me if they acknowledged it or validated me, as caring and expecting, would have just left me dependent on their response. At that point, to 'Me' - I was the only one who mattered... I was the only one who needed to acknowledge and validate 'Me', because it was about 'My,' growth and 'My' freedom. Priority and Importance must be given to 'Your' realisation, not theirs! When it's time for them to step outside of the matrix they will, but until then, they will continue finding hosts to feed them. Can you see how we are the ones making it hard for ourselves? Trying to maintain the master slave mentality in a roundabout way? If you are still wanting to give away your power by depending on someone to understand and acknowledge you, accept you, 'Love You', – you are still looking for approval, for your thoughts, your realisation and your growth. We should 'Never' give someone that much power over us! Accept your power for what it is... Yours! Be brave and wear It, become You! – realise that some are not meant to come with us.

Stop looking for the company of others that are not ready! Balance the male and female power within yourself, – Male being the doing part, and female the thinking part, Physical and Spiritual. Do not seek balance outside of yourself, it does not exist, everything you need is within! We are not a programme, we are consciousness, 'Spirit Housed' in a physical body. We are free, we are not a programme to be reset, and re- loaded over and over again! Observe your thoughts! Instead of thinking you need to action them, or rather feeling you need to action them like some sort of drug that your body needs in order to function. When you feel anxious let it ride over you, instead of reacting! – you 'Do Not' feed it in order for it to go away, – giving attention to it will actually be strengthening it… you don't need to be doing to feel as if you are functioning, – you don't need to be pleasing to feel as if you are accepted. The only acceptance needed is 'Your Own!'

In order to write this book, I needed to be of a certain mind-set, – if I hadn't overcome the battles in my life I wouldn't have been able to write at all. I figure that is why throughout my life I have been, and still am, constantly challenged. I am what you would call a 'True' modern-day warrior. When I say people in my life have tried to stop me writing, I meant it as in metaphorically, through custodian programming… as in, if their treatment of me had succeeded in fucking me up, I would not have been able to figure out what needed to be written, let alone write it, they had more to do with hampering and tampering with my sense of self, fucking up my confidence.

Trying to take me off my path by any means, whether spiritually or physically in many ways, – more than I care to mention. Whilst at the same time, I know their pursuit of me has been part of my journey, because they helped in providing me with what I needed to experience, in order to learn and 'Wake Up!' So, they have actually been good teachers, in that respect a double ended sword, for that I mildly thank them! The attacks both mentally and spiritually have only strengthened me, in order to enable me to clean their shit out of me, meaning, - to make space to impart and gain further knowledge. At the same time, I've felt tired, heavy and at times very alone, - all part of the process I know, pertaining to the road I chose to walk. I have so much to be thankful for, but being in constant growth can sometimes prevent the person from seeing or realising any of it, one develops a humbleness that surpasses any thoughts of specialness, That, I wouldn't change for anything. I am more 'Me' as a result. At times nothing feels like anything anymore, everything feels surreal, like an illusion… nothing feels real, I guess that's because it isn't. We need to feel love to withstand living here on earth, when we don't, we 'Must Love Our-Selves', although being Loved, teaches us how!

> "I Love My-Self, I Love Me,
> I Love the Creator of All Within Me".

The validation for the pain you have endured is held within - not without - in someone else. The thing happened to you, so only you can give you closure. To hold on to it in a hope that the person will give you relief, or release through words or actions, is willful abandonment of true self - yourself again! If that is you; then you are a person who is choosing to inflict it upon themselves through the memory of a learned behaviour, whereas before, someone was inflicting it upon you! them laying a foundation in order for you to stay in the denial of it, which concludes to being, only 'You' can free 'You!'

Letting go of your stuff is going to affect everything you are used to doing, (in a good way I might add) although at the time it may not feel that way, - that's because you will be unconsciously drawn to react in the opposite way in which you did before. Your challenge will be to see it through, no matter how uncomfortable and scary it feels, – uncomfortable because it feels right, (a new feeling you will need to get used to) and scary because the false fear of the consequences will be upon you! In fact, it is the fear that made you attach it to a feeling, of dread and consequence in the first place, - all subject to feeling threatened, whether passive or aggressive. If you dare to choose 'Your Self', you must remember that fear is just a feeling, it has no power unless you give power to it.

Remaining in a relationship, place or situation where the dynamic is to drain your energy, is far more damaging to you than fearing a consequence of someone's response, just because it maybe in a way that you won't like, however, when you are truly ready to let go of a toxic relationship, you won't give a shit about consequences, you will just want to get away! Be Free! You reacting in the opposite way to what they are used to; will weaken the basis for which they are accustomed to draining you, it will take away the power you gave them to use against you, - merely because they are not expecting your boundaries to be raised, or for you to respond. You will also regain the power you had given them. Unconscious non-action will leave you stuck, you must do the work - the work is to watch your own back! No longer allow yourself to be in sacrifice to another's emotions or to another's projected fears! It will confine you not only to a space/environment, but to them. Anything that puts you into a feeling of victim mentality, that makes you feel you have no control over your life or being, will stunt and block you, keep you on the mouse wheel. You must not hold yourself back for people because that is where deception of self happens. You begin to see only what you choose to see (selective visual attention) pertaining to your deception - not what is really happening! along with selective hearing, 'Not' what is really being said! People project their own fears and shadows onto each other, – the unhealed part of their psyche, their own issues onto you, because they don't want to deal with it, or are too scared to face it along with the consequences from it, so they deny it within themselves, thus choose to see it in you, accusing you and blaming you for behaviours and attitudes that they are displaying, yet unaware of.

It not only gives them a false sense of validation with regards to the notion of it being you, - your fault etc. It also aids in the fueling of their own deception, safely keeping the awareness of 'Self' hidden, leaving them to remain in denial, programmed into the matrix. Please know that a lot of people who are toxic, or in toxic situations do not move, or get themselves out of them, - simply because they don't want to! Get out of the way! Trying to help them change and grow is futile, they will fight you to stay the way they are! Holding you in a regressive frame of mind with them, because they are comfortable within the discomfort, so be mindful, the intention is to keep you there as an accomplice to offload upon, colluding with them to serve as conformation to their delusions and beliefs as mentioned earlier in the book. Do not sit in any situation that hampers your understanding of self, - thus spiritual advancement, regardless of your attachment to them. Changing your out-put is the only way growth can be obtained, learn to stop picking other people's pieces up! Part of that growth is to 'Not' feel attracted to your usual debilitating habits, when this is accomplished it means that you have severed the need to experience them.

When I come up against a fear, I find myself writing down exactly how I feel, allowing myself to express whatever emotion comes up, along with the accompanying thoughts that go with it. 'I do Not' sensor what I am writing (I just write whatever comes up). I realise that I am dissipating them as I write, then after a short time I notice space in my energy, clear where that emotion thought once lived. It has no more hold over me, nothing, no thing is any longer there! just space, – the magnetized attachment is gone. This space gives you the clarity to see what affect the situations, people, and lack of boundaries were having on your ability to validate yourself and grow, thus allowing you to make better choices! It's about realising what you do, then feeling what happens to your energy as a result, it's about noticing the negative debilitating emotions, that have been placed upon you, that have been blocking you and regressing you, keeping you stuck, - then choosing to no longer feed it or let it happen to you. In the Celestine Prophecy it was called an energy game, drama or dynamic, – the thing people do to extract energy from others and vice versa. This is about getting past the need to do that, to take responsibility for yourself, instead of passing your bullshit on to others. It is about letting go of the need to be right, or helpful or anything that is not productive to your well- being. Result being, self-depreciation, stagnation, more drama and attachments. Conscious non-reaction, – staying with your own energy/feelings, allowing yourself to see and sense what is behind it, (the root) instead of giving realisation of it away.

You will naturally stop self- sabotaging when you start to see, feel and experience what the payoff is… it's all part of the process, you will actually look brighter, be energetically lighter as opposed to feeling heavy, and appear slimmer because you are! When you make the choice to no longer attach yourself to pain, inherited and otherwise, along with family ties and people who drain you, you will start to lose weight, especially on your stomach, which is significant, because weight carried on the body is a physical manifestation of the issues we hold inside, (as above so below, - as within so without) The stomach is where we carry. The solar plexus, which is where the intuition resides, is also where a lot of our blockages live, – I could mention constipation at this point! However, whilst at the same time it is within the solar plexus chakra that we receive psychic and sensual information, the gut feeling, it is also the part of us prone to attack from outside entities, (people) who wish us harm, and people who want to offload their shit, all in the form of judgements, fears, hostility, denials and criticisms – all projections!

When you have an uncomfortable feeling in your stomach, or any other part of your body I might add, relax and release! Allow yourself to feel it, – do not hold on to it, or resist it by actively finding something else to do, – as it may take a while for it to re-surface again. You are experiencing your process, you must take advantage of this and see it as an opportunity to clear some baggage, it is a gift, let it happen!

Whatever issue is attached, will come up for you at the same time, to be understood then dissipated, be still and listen, – just let go! When you have done this a few times, you will also find that the things you used to react to, are no longer a cause for concern, or even a reactive trigger in you. The position they previously took, will be replaced with calm, open emptiness in the form of space. The more you allow yourself to do this (let go) the lighter you will become. You will also be storing your energy instead of giving it away, this is in order to gather enough resilience for the next time you are being challenged. Remember, 'Energy Is Resilience!' We must learn to hold on to it!

# Principle {11}

If you make the decision to let go of a person, situation or behavior, that you have already intuited as holding you back... then backtrack. You will ultimately be led back into the mess and debris of the constructed emotions of the false self. Thus, you will continue to become triggered by self- debilitating thoughts, to once again become a victim to the harmful desires and addictions, that once left you blocked and blinded in the first place. It will also be a little harder to release the emotions this time, because the constructed self will fight harder to convince you that you are making a mistake. It does this by throwing up all manner of thought and feelings to tempt you in order to drag you back. However, it is a double ended sword, if you are sensitive enough to see the positive aspect as being: you haven't yet built up enough resilience to break that particular cycle.

"You are being led back into the lesson as an opportunity for it to be learnt". Leading you back is deliberate, in order to manifest more of the same situations until you get it! However, your eventual freedom is assured, - if you had previously harvested some energy (resilience) from before, by reacting in the opposite fashion. Payoff being, the time spent in regression will be shorter, because your newly stored foundational energy will automatically pull you towards it, you will then be reminded of what feels good, in comparison to the discomfort, previously endured by the constructed emotions for which you will now become repelled by. Once you embrace this sense of what happened to regress, - you will unfold, you will then become unattached from the connective trigger of the leading toxic situation, - as it outlines the reason for having been placed there in the first place. This is your unresolved issue! A hole can never keep you inside it once you have found the ladder out, metaphorically speaking. As you begin the work of self-realisation, your harvested energy turns into your personal stash of self-worth and forgiveness, further solidifying your connection with your 'You!' We don't always get it the first time around, even when we pertain to know better! Part of the process is to solidify self- awareness, 'boundaries' through repetition, till it's 'GOT!' Once you've seen a 'thing', it therefore 'is', hence why you must not go back on your word or intuition, no matter what form the temptation takes, pay attention! The emotion, 'Attachment' will always try and drag you back!

You must always walk forward, lest you meet hazard and instability - you will become unstable. Easier said than done, I know, because I've been encountering pull back continually as I write this book, and although never giving up, (which is Not an option!) I am experiencing countless interference, and a heaviness that is indescribable. To me, my body feels like I'm carting around a concrete boulder, – you could say the devil has been tracking me and trying to ride my back all the way! It has only been through a necessity to stay awake that I am able to continue, and a knowing that without a doubt my job is to aid others to do the same. Become aware to stay 'Awake'.

# Carrying Anothers Cross

Her only problem is her dad, – every other issue she has, derived from that. His lack of emotional support, his distorted feelings towards her when she was born, his lack of care for her, not ever taking accountability or understanding of what he has done to her, has crushed her! He continues to tell people she is crazy. Every time he walks into her life another nail is added to her coffin. He is fully aware of twisting the love she has for him, to the point where she is willing to destroy herself in the hope that he will finally rescue her, - say Sorry! Something, to take away the pain that he created in her. Because it never comes, instead she chooses men (passive aggressive) that match the toxic intensity he transferred to the little girl in her, as a false representation of love, leaving it inside her as her only reference.

Her mother not there to protect her, even when she was alive, encouraged a loneliness to ensue, accompanied by a hole in her soul that mother would have filled. Unfortunately, just like her mother, she will probably die, due to the amount of alcohol she depends on every day in order to numb herself, and lock away her heart from further being torn apart by the guilt, – his guilt, that he placed upon her innocent soul, making it impossible for her to see it wasn't her fault. She, controlling everyone around her, with her toxic projections of unhealed over- caution, created from his abuse, continually creating carnage and mental instability in the lives of her children, thus silencing their intuition, preventing them from confiding in her, due to not being able to build a healthy foundation in herself, or in them, in which they can walk. All she has to do is let go of the notion that the father figure in her life is her saviour, - she has to let go of the belief, that she has a responsibility to uphold a loyalty, that allows him access to her, although he has destroyed her, - just because he, by blood is her dad. She, consumed by a mixed up confused fairy-tale! The confusion she felt as a child when he took advantage of her trust for him, - naturally wanting to be close to him, (like safe fathers are with their daughters), was turned into a mental mind game of secrets and toxic destruction; albeit, a 'Pleasure' for him. She became mixed up, her self-worth hidden under a false sense of loyalty, wrapped in guilt, his guilt! His guilt his 'Shadow' became placed upon her. His toxic emotions govern her, through transference of his warped confusion of her, as his desire, Sickening! It 'sickened her!' to be translated in her mind masked as love.

He uses her love for him to control her, along with her innocent nature, she became eager to please... this is the continuous cycle she is trapped in. Her ability to tap into her self-awareness has been blocked, somewhere inside she believes she can't get out. The alcohol, along with his grooming has successfully clouded her judgment, thus, refusing her entry to much needed memories to accompany the realisation of crimes done to her. She has become locked down, assisted by her alcoholic haze, as the hole widens. Emotions left with no opportunity to dissipate because of her father's lack of accountability, and responsibility for her pain. She has no love for herself, no interest in seeking spiritual retribution, or becoming self-aware. She has no peace, and seems to prefer to wallow in an intoxicated mess. He, her father, has made his cross, - Her cross to bear. Therefore! The devil custodian energy wins! Successfully harnessing the lifeforce of her soul.

# Realisation Before It's Too Late

If you truly want to, you can get out Precious Butterfly, as your story is slightly different. As a little girl you loved your dad unconditionally. He, jealous of the attention you received from your mother; Jealous, like when his own brother was born, 'Jealous of him', when his brother was a baby, he put him in a skip, tried to throw him away. So, when you were born, would disregard you. Your Mother once leaving you too! Although you were 'Never' starved of her love, the short time apart also affected you. Although she was there for you, would tell you she loved you every day, damage was already done. A lack in you, was the disowning by your dad, somehow, he managed to put guilt into you. As a teenager you accepted him and did your best to show him who you are - that you exist, - he simply chose to refuse to see! Understand that it is 'Not' your fault. His inability to see himself, forbids him from seeing 'You'. As a result, lack of self-worth became your issue, your Attachment, this creating a hole and gap in you.

You then felt it your responsibility, to try and prove your worth to him. However, He continues to disregard you, leaving you distraught every time. Vulnerable, trying to escape distress, you made yourself available to a remedy of substitute bindings, which teases you towards destruction. Butterfly, know that your self-worth is inherent in you, it is a birth right, it has nothing to do with him! You keep his disregard of you alive, by the attention you give to his absence. Allowing him, like narcissistic supply, - to syphon the energy you have cultivated for yourself, to fill the gap he created. Unconsciously, you are allowing him to feed from the want for 'Him' in you, grateful whenever he appears in your life. As he hasn't, the gap in you, lonely for his love, a fathers love. You attract substitutes with empty minds, not being a match to your intelligence, to be the father. Like him, they feed from your need, In order to build themselves up, harnessing your energy, to fill the gaps in them, draining you. You, not allowing yourself to cultivate resilience... Not allowing yourself to come up for air. You allow the substitute to constantly lead you to self- depreciation, the projection in them. The custodian cleverly utilizes the want for dad, sticking lack of self-worth to you, like bubblegum, hard to remove. He, your dad, as long as he can keep you in a mental untruth, of believing you need something from him, in order to be whole, you will remain stuck! He, dangling himself like a carrot that you can never reach. Therefore, 'You' as a source of energy supply is all he will ever see.

Because he is empty; he takes advantage of your lack of his presence. He fully knows who you are! He also knows that when he comes into your life his destructive vibration becomes yours, just as your unconditional love becomes his, like the substitute, it is his way of feeling a semblance of all that he is not! Like a true narcissist. That is why you are always left feeling deprived, lacking confidence, drained and self-hating, – those are his feelings towards himself, his vibration, his projection, – Not yours!

Self-Awareness will give you courage and determination! energetically choose to change your mind, - Cut the Need Off! realise that it has Never made you feel good! You do not deserve to remain dead with him, you walk on dangerous ground. Feeling the need and desire to buy alcohol, is showing you what your shadow aspect feeds from, the part of you the custodian uses to entice you in order to destroy you, and take your life force. Like the substitute, It is no coincidence that your dad appears just as you are about to turn a corner in your life, whether that is physically, in your mind as a thought, or manifest in the energy of another, who's intent is to remind you to feel disregarded, and worthless; this is the way the substitute solidifies their place in your life. You are ready to ascend on to your path and reason for being here. Butterfly, there is no one to blame for you not taking steps forward, once you know the cause of your delay. No one can dismiss your dad for you, the energy required for that must come from you! In the act of letting go, you will claim and take back all the energy life force he has syphoned from you. By law (universal spiritual law), it will be returned to you.

It will be returned because you are choosing 'You!' It will be returned because you will then have learnt to become discerning! Responsibility is to 'Your-Self!' You are not here to appease him, his vibration or anybody else, drop the loyalty you have to a fairytale! You have been unconsciously seeking others, to match the intensity of the disregard you constantly experienced from him as a child, - given to you to carry, as your anchor to the matrix, along with the contempt you have for yourself...

Butterfly you just have a little way to go, - your wings are still intact, you only need to choose which side you are on, – Yours, or the custodian entity, who is currently trying to take up permanent residency in you, in order to syphon the life force from you, through the attachment of self- debilitation, and guilt that does 'Not' belong to you. This is the choice 'We' are constantly being called to make. Release the attachment, it does 'Not' belong to you! or serve you! The darkness put upon you is 'Not' your cross to bear! You must free yourself from the guilt projected on to you. Claim back the energy that is yours. One day you will wake up having had enough! Then you will have the courage, to let go and allow yourself to feel the pain. Your trapped energy, hidden under the pain is golden, it contains your confidence., releasing it, is your way out! Overcoming this fork on your road, is one of the reasons your are here. When the pain comes up, choose to become discerning! become the observer instead of the casualty, allow the thoughts and beliefs attached to sail past you and dissipate, do Not try to catch any of them, do Not relate to them! View them as temptations, trying to get you to take them. The Power you hold within You is stronger than them!

The 'Value' we Receive from others, is Matched by the 'Value' (We) have for Our-Selves!

We must become aware of the positive meaning within a potentially invasive energy, – then transmute the self- debasing thoughts that come towards us from it. We must ask ourselves, 'Why' is it happening, and 'Who' does it serve? 'What' does it serve? because it isn't you! We are then able to claim back energy that belongs to us, and let go of what doesn't. The invasive energy will naturally return to sender, – you will feel a difference as it naturally dissipates. Everything damning within a situation is for the purpose of strengthening us up. Although we fall into the trap of denial, everything is really structured to lead us back towards Self, and subsequently 'Home!' Good luck will at times come disguised as bad. You must start to look at things through a higher perspective.

If someone is absolutely brutal and repulsive towards you, and you are conscious of this, but you still expect them to one day change, or behave differently towards you. Continuously giving them the benefit of doubt, thus chance after chance, believing they will become someone, they clearly are not. By continuing to remain surprised when they don't stop, and instead choosing to endure it. Then, how they continue to treat you - is your own fault! because you already knew! - hence, you have become the enabler. Understand that, 'No' amount of self-sacrifice will ever be enough! when they have drained you, they will move onto someone else!

Learn to respect yourself and the choice they have made to be like that, and walk away. They are stagnating your life! Allow them to implode at their own peril - It is 'Not' your job to rescue them, try to change them or withstand them! You staying and being a cushion for them is actually delaying their growth, preventing consequences that they have willfully earned, along with important lessons they need to learn. When they have had enough consequences, they will stop, Or Not! whatever happens - is not your cross to bear.

Our lives are a game of chess, two opposing energies in opposite polarity to each other. In the grand scheme of things, we, as pawns are being maneuvered around the board by reflection of the choices we make, dependent on how much pain, fear and self-deception we choose to hold on to. If we choose the way of fear, attachments and blindness, we are fucked, our soul's life force remains the property of the custodian, harvested due to us not claiming it as ours, - destined to continually bounce from lifetime to lifetime, merely existing until we wake up. However, if we are brave enough to walk the way of self-awareness, we release our soul from captivity, then 'Freedom' ensues! Become self-reliant, devoid of pain, representative of change, Not a Things property! The choice is always ours, – We just need to know – choice exists! Don't believe what you believe just because they told you! Introspection is always needed until you have solidified Self-Awareness.

We dissipate negative energy, – energy that doesn't belong to us, by becoming discerning towards it, no matter how energetically tempting it becomes, – 'watch the thoughts go by', instead of becoming them. If you choose to let them overcome you, by triggering you through relating to them, – you would be unnecessarily holding on to them. Remember! They are an energy vibration, that came into you from outside of you, they are not actually you! Choose to change your mind, it's as simple as that! When you give in to the notion of the energy attached to the thought as being real, you are feeding it. When you see yourself as a victim of it you are feeding it, it is only a construct, an entity encouraging you to believe in its existence, to believe that you need it. This is an illusion, it has no real power apart from the power in the energy you give it, through your attention and association with the story it tells. Knowledge is what feeds your being, – understanding is your true power! Choose to change your mind, and then let go! You can actually change your mind, and choose not to invest your energy into negative feelings or words any more. Some will say 'that's just the way they are'… well, it is NOT! The words were never yours in the first place, so why, - for argument's sake do you happily assume ownership of them? In fact! why are you holding on to them? The illusion you are under, is that they are 'You', inside you, - they are Not! They are outside of you, they are not 'You', regardless of what you experienced as a result of their attachment, (Attachment) being the operative word! At the end of the day it's your choice, it is always your choice, always has been! You just didn't know it! I'm not saying to pretend nothing ever happened to you, I am not saying to block the hurt or pain, – I'm saying to choose to no longer wear the experiences as your cloak, because the cloak never belonged to you in the first place.

Trauma is an attachment so give it back! By refusing to relate to it in the face of any adversity you may be currently experiencing or have experienced, by not investing any energy attention into the emotion, - learn to not bite! To deny you are the emotion denies access to the power you are used to giving it by associating with it, Yes allow yourself to feel it then 'Let Go', – it will then dissipate. At this point, I also want to mention that in my everyday life, I notice that I cannot do what I don't have allotted energy for, - in the past I have reasoned that I'm not supposed to do that particular thing, or action then! Especially if I've been drained! However, when I began to harvest my energy, I later learnt that when I am supposed to do a particular thing or action, the esteem and energy comes to accompany the idea of it. If I try to do it without allotted energy, it becomes difficult and tiring, like I'm going against a current rather than flowing with it. I actually feel my energy lower, and body feel heavy in protest as a sign, then as a result it not only takes longer but isn't done so well. On the other hand, when I am supposed to do something, I race through quick time, enjoying it! it becomes therapeutic, I am energised from it. When something is supposed to be, it is simple, it flows, a sense of surety accompanies it. We harvest energy from doing the right thing at the right time!

The closer you get to your destination the more ruthless the opposing energy gets. It will use whoever is closest to you to try and destroy your sense of connection to self, to knock you off the path. As you heal and grow, it will try to place guilt onto you, to block you as it has nothing left to latch itself onto, - so it will try to create mess to discredit you in the minds of those you love and trust, to further increase a sense of alone. This it relies on, - to coax and drag you back into believing unhealthy emotions and thoughts belong to you.

Every historical loose end of yours is going to swing back at you, in order to be tied up and dissipated, although at the time it will feel as if it is destroying you. The things you thought you took care of, and did your best to accommodate, at the time in a responsible way, according to the mind set you had, will come back to you to haunt you! If you created any holes in someone that turned out to be a boulder that binds them, this is the time you will know about it. They will appear as 'hard to swallow pills', that you will choke on, if you have not cultivated enough reserve (harvested) energy of self-worth and forgiveness. Accusations towards you will appear just at the point of you turning a corner, in an attempt to floor you! At these times you are called to take accountability and acknowledge the part you played, along with being given an opportunity to relay your own innocence, in order to stay in the truth with regards to your intent concerning whatever action you took at that time, this being assurance from you that it was done to cause no harm.

I say this because 'you' will know what the truth is purely based on the assumption that you were there. It being you, that made the certain decisions so you know what you were feeling at the time, therefore, you know your true intent! I will highlight the fact that my use of the word 'innocence' is only relating to whether at the time you would've been coming from a place of love and not malice, (if you were, then you must take accountability!) We damage others by 'Not' taking responsibility for what we have done - thus prolonging the attachment to the negative energy for both you and them. However, the other side of this is; We must only accept and hold ourselves accountable for what is true, – not because someone gives us their perception, which isn't always going to be based on our true intent, but instead, based on the way they see it, but still expect us to go along with it, because it validates a need in them to justify their own behaviors, - if negative, with regards to the direction their life went as a result. Their narrative will generally be steeped in blame, taking no responsibility for the part they are playing in preventing themselves from growing and healing as the now adult, basically, you will be told it is your fault! If we give in to this, they will then be syphoning our energy, life force, through the guilt and blame that they have successfully attached to us. I will now say that; even if you take responsibility and accountability for the part you played in creating the hole, this does not prevent the person from using the situation as a crutch, choosing instead to stay there and wallow, - result being, we then become their scapegoat.

As the scapegoat, we need to protect our own energy, by not accepting projections, or scenarios that have been created by another, then used against us, - with demands that we own them, especially when we know the perception, projection is not true. At the same time with consideration for the outcome of our original decision, although having not being our intention, meaning; although we did not intentionally mean to cause that effect, we still need to take accountability for the 'part we played'.

As the scapegoat, forgiving yourself first, then letting go, will shield you from any guilt that is trying to enter. Forgiveness works by harnessing your energy, (bringing it back to you) like a psychological armour, in preparation to withstand blame and fear of consequence. Building yourself up, in order to form the vibration needed to exercise condition-less empathy. Instead of energetically running away in fear of losing energy, you will be choosing to create a stance of walking in another's shoes! It is then that you will discover that there is 'Nothing' to lose but only to gain! you will also get to feel lighter as a result, also, the person afflicted will be given the awareness to heal faster, or choose to find someone else to blame, – whatever direction they choose will be theirs until they are ready to grow!

Although we will be faced with fault for the hole, and the consequence to the person's life as a result of the hole being there, chances are, at the time, the choices we made were believed to be the best, and only ones we could make with the mindset we had! Now, however, an apology and validation are needed for making them in the first place. Honesty, and ownership of said choice are needed to set us and them free, whether or not they choose to hold on to it. You may find that the pain you haven't been able to let go of isn't coming from the place you first thought, but from a hole you once created in someone that you didn't know you were responsible for making, what you are feeling is their projection. At the time, the person needed you to be fully spiritually and energetically present, to make an informed decision, protect them from harm and guide them. However, it is to be understood that you had already been taken yourself, damaged programmed and dampened, thus perception was through the mask, the ego false self. Ask yourself for Forgiveness! whether you truly feel it or not. Whether the person chooses to let go of it or not is none of your concern, as the gift, is in 'you' seeing 'your' error. Only then will you be able to begin to truly forgive yourself. The devil/custodian, loves to use these historical holes to fuck us up! to prevent us and the person involved from going towards the next stage of growth.

Forgiving, taking accountability, letting go and releasing your attachment to the energy of a situation, releases it on other dimensions. The double ended sword is that although painful, everyone will eventually get what they need as a result, as in - it was another meant to be situation pertaining to 'Unfinished Business', as nothing can be left behind. Rest assured you will duly get up, dust yourself down, and continue to walk! not forgetting to Thank the dealer for the illusionary trump card played!

Remember: "Love and Gratitude Always!"

# Other Worlds

It is with a kind of difficulty and apprehension that I write what I'm going to write next, however, I am being led to share some of it... well, only what is necessary! The rest will go into another book... Maybe!

I say difficulty, because this is unlike everything else I have told you. It is different in a sense that, it isn't going to be easy to translate in a way that can be as easily understood, or digested like the other stuff, - But that's only because, you may have already deliberately refused to see for yourselves what I'm about to say, through fear of it, so will not acknowledge that it exists. And apprehension, because I feel I am extremely privileged to have been shown what I'm going to tell you, - what I've seen, sensed and experienced- so it's mine! Experiences that I thought belonged to me, So, feel reluctant to tell you.

Not only that, I will be holding myself open to scrutiny or attack (whichever your poison), on something that I know to be real, and something I don't care to have to prove, convince or explain to anybody, because part of me doesn't think I should have to, - reason being, you should already know! However, I need to share it with you in order to tie this whole book together. With that said, it is up to you what memories you decide to uncover for yourselves in relation to this, I will even go as far to say, that I guess my job is to humbly remind you. Now, let's continue shall we! I say - reluctantly…

I have been tracked all my life, I have been surrounded by people and entities who have willfully, and deliberately tried to prevent my realisation. I have also been under attack, although it wasn't obvious, in hindsight, that's because I have also been too trusting! However, throughout I have been protected and accompanied all the way. I can also say that everything I have ever experienced has been part of my journey and training, all of which was necessary, in order for me to wake up, as someone had to shovel the shit for others to enable them to have a clear road, - so I guess that someone is me! I must also say I wouldn't have it any other way, although if asked whilst certain things were happening, I would've said, and did say, albeit to myself; why me? It's not fair, and for fuck sake let me come up for air sometimes why don't you! With that said, 'Why Not Me!' Being 'Me' hasn't been easy but worth every minute, second, century and eon.

I recall at around 3 years of age seeing my mother's boots moving up and down the bedroom wall in unison, from otherwise standing stationary. They first parted from standing together as a pair, and stationed themselves one at each end of the wall, then as one went up the other would come down, but never did they both go up or down together at the same time, but in time if you know what I mean. At the time, as I watched, I wondered what was happening, but wasn't scared, and didn't think it unusual, just entertaining. As an adult, I realise that it was me moving them telekinetically.

When I was a little older, I lay in bed, then suddenly, directly opposite me at the foot of my bed, a tall figure appeared wearing a long black coat and a wide brimmed black hat, a face wasn't noticeable, maybe because my curiosity wouldn't allow my eyes to inspect it. I am also reluctant to say it was male, but do so just because of what it was wearing, - it wasn't in shadow form it looked solid 3 dimensional. At the time it was light outside, summertime, early evening when it happened, as I used to go to bed around 6pm, so saw clearly what I saw. I recall feeling uncomfortable, so I promptly covered my head with my blanket and lay as still as I could, not making a sound, not even wanting to breathe, in case it heard me. Although it felt like ages, I don't actually know how long it had been there, and I didn't know what it was, but at the same time I did (if that makes any sense), because I felt familiar with its energy. I have never forgotten what I saw that day, - I haven't been permitted to! Like a lot of the things I have seen.

I don't think I was actually in any danger either, it just felt to be staring at me. In hindsight, I truly believe it was watching over me, to protect me from some form of spiritual attack maybe? - more than likely, - although it could've just been checking up on me. I chose to cover my head under my blanket until it had disappeared. I sensed no movement from it in my room, however, from under my cover, just a sense of its presence. The best way to describe the feeling was; although I had a blanket over me, the blanket felt like it was transparent, the only way I knew it was covering me was because my body felt a slight weight from it. Other than that, I felt exposed and weightless, like it could see through me, light as a feather, no fear just exposed like I had no body or covering. After seeing the tall form in my bedroom, I had become frightened of the dark, although I had seen it when it was light, I didn't see it again but kept sensing that something was watching me, or standing over me, as I could sense energy other than my own in my room with me. The winter months were the worse because it became dark earlier, I would cover my head under my blanket leaving a tiny gap to breathe, cocooned and sweating, feeling so hot but not moving, wishing for morning to come. As an adult, my cousin Joan who at that time would come and stay with us when I was a child, told me that every time she came over she would see a very tall dark figure standing over me at the side of my bed. From where her bed was positioned it had its back to her, she said it would stare at me, just watching me as I slept. She described it as a silhouette of a man, – it wasn't wearing a hat, so I can't say it was the same figure that I saw. Strange how I had kept that to myself.

When I was at primary school, in the summer, during playtime, I would sometimes lay on my stomach on the school field, and feel vibrational tremors beneath me, coming up from the earth, and through my entire body! It felt so strange, so intense and powerful, whilst at the same time energising and engaging, my child mind actually believed the grassy earth would tip and I would fall off, so I would grip onto the grass with my hands. Those memories are now what I use to centre myself when under attack, - The hot sunny days were in fact my connection to the earth. I also read the other day about babies, always lifting their legs up in protest through not wanting to be put on the grass, and immediately I thought it was because they can feel the vibrational energy from the earth coming through, and probably feels a bit much for them, considering they have just got here.

When the neighbour who lived opposite killed his wife, I remember looking out of the window into the street, police standing outside his house, and feeling a heavy vibration go through my body, - hearing a loud thunderous deep tone, which coldly boomed exactly 3 times, it wasn't audible to anyone else just me. I believe it was the vibration of a 'passing over' to the spirit realm. The tone, sinister, and eerie in nature, likened to the sub bass drum of a state funeral. I was left feeling shaky and haunted, - almost imposed upon for days, with a fear of the husband coming to get me. I managed to put those experiences out of my mind as I grew.

When I reached my early teenage years, I remember having a sleepover at my then best friend's house. We were top to tail in her bed, when my body became overwhelmingly heavy, as if I was being held down but from the inside of my skin. It was trance like, I couldn't move, I had my eyes open but couldn't speak, couldn't move my head to look at what was on top of me. My mind, well, consciousness is all I had the use of! Then something said recite the lord's prayer. When I did this in my mind, the heaviness released me! At that point I immediately sat up, told my friend and asked if she had felt it, or saw anything, - she said no. That was the start of what I call random jump on's, which I later understood to be disembodied spirits, landing on me, cloaking my body with their shadow, which rendered my body immobile! They, attempting to momentarily re-live the experience of being in a vessel. Me being empathic and naturally high vibrational, at the time with no direction, –so, was wide open. Those spirits were the ones I eventually learnt to send towards the light. I've since discovered through experience that the lord's prayer worked because the spirits were once earthbound, they obviously believed in the doctrines of the bible, so feared what I recited and fled. However, just to let you know, the same prayer doesn't work on entities.

As an adult, I've seen and continue to see a lot of what could be perceived to be otherworldly, however, I am no longer scared of the dark, and no longer feel threatened by spirits or otherworldly existence, visitations or entities. Although, sometimes I'm still surprised due to not having anticipated it coming, - 'it', as in alternate vibrations, but mostly I'm blended because I know it means me no harm, neither can it do any harm. With that said, I know it is here, or their, whichever way you choose to comprehend it, - I know it is real.

Sharon... I went to lay on my bed on my back one afternoon, after having had a bath with the towel wrapped around me. With what felt like momentarily closing my eyes, to then land on my forehead, on the floor at the foot of my bed with a bang! I then raised myself up to then hear the phone ringing. I got up slightly dazed and walked down the stairs to answer it. Above where I had my phone is a mirror, when I looked at myself I saw that a triangle had been cut out of the left side of my head, over an area that I later found out to be, are my hypothalamus and pituitary glands. The wound was a fleshy light pink, no blood no pain, a little achy, but that was all. I was left in a daze but ok. The bang on the centre of my forehead did not hurt and was not swollen, neither did it have any sign of an impact, which was strange considering I had just landed on it. The wound to the left of my head healed really quickly. In less than a week my skin had regenerated and was back covering, only leaving a shadow of the cut, which I still have on the left side of my head today, although faint you can still see it.

I have no recollection of where I went but I know I went somewhere, I know that something had been done, some kind of operation had been performed! I also think it was stopped before they could finish off, hence why the wound was still visible when I landed, the phone ringing must have interrupted them before my skin had a chance to completely knit itself back together, or maybe I was just supposed to see it? I also noticed that my awareness had become heightened after the experience, – I have a photo of me taken at my sister's birthday party a little over a week after it happened.

Again, I lay on my bed one early afternoon just having gotten out of the bath, relaxed and skim reading a magazine. As I lay I began to feel unusual so I got up, but instead of getting up, 'I', got up, - meaning I somehow came up out of my body. Shocked at this I quickly lay back in, thinking the unusual feeling would go and I would return into my body. Then attempted to get up again, but the same thing happened, this time slightly alarming me. On the third attempt to get up, - whatever apprehension I was feeling had gone. I had now become used to the odd feeling, so decided to just get up, I then turned and saw my physical body lying on my bed and thought nothing of it! By this time the notion of being out of my body felt familiar and kind of normal, like I had done it before but just had no recollection.

Everything in my room looked the same, identical! The chest of drawers which stood directly opposite my bed, against the wall were the same, everything looked the same! My bedroom door was open and in the same place, so I decided to explore and went into my daughter's bedroom, and immediately noticed the curtains were closed, – I thought this was strange because I know they were open as it was afternoon. I went over to them and opened them, - the shock of then looking out of the window to see that it was velvet pitch black outside! Nothing! This shook me back into my body. - With that, I sat up on my bed in disbelief at what had just taken place. – Apart from having what is coined as an outer body experience, why in that dimension was my home seeming to be floating in a pitch-black abyss, duplicate to the home my physical lived in, but on a parallel dimension? Gosh! I was just in a parallel dimension, what the fuck! My only regret was not looking down at the form I took whilst out of my body, as it would have been interesting to see what I looked like.

Another time, I was in my daughter's room laying on her floor chilling, she was up on her bunk-type-bed colouring. Above her on her ceiling I had hung a kite mobile, it had long colourful strips of crepe paper hanging from it, forming a tail, anyway, for some reason I closed my eyes and found myself out of my body, it was almost instant. At this point I didn't know how I was doing it? I just did it! I elevated to the bunkbed, and moved the mobile's dangly bits for a while, I guess by manipulating the energy around it, - but to me I was blowing it, then before I knew it, I found myself traveling on a kind of moving floor conveyer belt type thing. The surroundings felt like a cave, but it wasn't, because the sides of it were smooth but thick and metal like. I was in a narrow tunnel, with large spot lights above, - bedded into the metal ceiling, vertically along the length of the upper limit in a straight line, the place was matt gun metal grey in colour. As the belt moved me further along, I noticed to the right of me a glassed off compartment, which was cut in to the side of the tunnel. The glass window was about 6ft wide by 4ft high, not floor to ceiling - it was sitting on about 110cm of metal wall. Behind the glass screen were computers and monitors on the walls, lots of knobs, some were lit up some were not, the sort you would see in a live broadcasting production room. There were some computers backed up against the glass window, on a kind of control desk with what seemed to be people operating them, one was a woman, all wearing slightly lighter grey fitted uniforms, - well, they appeared to resemble people, humans, which I thought was strange, (what were, what looked like humans doing there?)

They looked alarmed to see me, like I wasn't supposed to be there! As I moved along on the belt, ahead I could see light, with outlines of 5 people standing within it. I also began to feel a pull towards them as in a familiarity, but before I could get any closer to them, I began to feel a sharp, tight squeezing pain on the middle of my left thumb, then was back in my body, in my daughters room, with her just as I had left her on her bed colouring. With my thumb still aching, I sat up and asked her if she had noticed anything unusual about her kite, and she told me the strips had been moving. The aching in my thumb lasted quite a while, I guess to make sure I didn't forget. My daughter is now an adult, and to this day she still remembers the day the kite moved!

I was at my friend's house with my then little girl. As she played in another room with my friends' child - we were in the kitchen standing across from each other in deep conversation, when all of a sudden and with such force, I was flung into her. As this happened I grabbed both of her hands, held on to them and squeezed, - at the same time I saw a vision of 7 tall figures standing sideways to me, on a black and white chequered floor, facing forwards, with another one at the front facing them. They all wore long hooded shrouds that concealed their bodies, - at that moment I thought what do they feel like? Then In lightning speed, and still standing sideways one of them was right in front of my face, - I could then see clearly that they felt like bark, the shrouds were made of bark! The colour was of real greens, real browns really rich in tone. - The colours on the earth plane are slightly diluted in comparison. With that, - I found myself back in my friends' kitchen, we all but shoved each other off to separate. When I released her hands, one of the rings she was wearing had literally bent out of shape, into her finger where I had squeezed it so tight with such force. It was a thick solid silver ring, – so to have bent that out of shape, would've taken a lot of strength and force (life force energy). We had initially let out a screech with shock, which brought our children running in to the kitchen to see what was wrong, we didn't know what the fuck had just happened! After talking and comparing mental notes we established that we had both seen the same thing, except my friend hadn't wandered any questions, so nothing more than figures standing facing the front with the one facing them, is all she was shown, at the time I drew a picture of them, Not, that I could Ever forget!

# PRINCIPLE {12}

My gifts have shown themselves to me in the strangest of ways! The day I walked past two strangers, a couple, however, on this particular day, as I literally crossed paths, with the woman on my left side, I clearly heard in my head, 'Look at the nigga'. It wasn't what she thought that surprised me, because I couldn't give a shit, - it was how I managed to pick it up, and hear it in the first place? It was at that moment that I knew I could pick up on another's thoughts.

I needed to understand what was happening to me, what these experiences meant, so that I could better deal with them and attempt to be more in control of them.

The first question I was driven to ask is what is spontaneous combustion? I had seen an old photograph of a woman sitting on a chair that fascinated me. She was surrounded by ash, her middle torso was obliterated, leaving the rest of her body parts smoking but intact. The chair she sat on, along with the room she was found in was untouched, neither was it scorched. It was obvious that the fire had started inside of her, my curiosity would not let go of the need to understand how this was possible! My next step was the library. I came out with not only a book on the subject, but also for some reason, Egyptian hieroglyphs became of interest. I learnt that from a spiritual point of view, spontaneous human combustion, is what happens when our energy meridians, (which are considered to be the passageways through which our energy flows) have not been sufficiently purged of negative energy. Throughout the bodies system, upon the kundalini rising and meeting its opposite, a chemical reaction is then sparked by the opposing energy, thus destruction occurs and ignites the body from inside. If spontaneous combustion does not occur as a result, the person will instead be rendered mentally and spiritually confused, left in a form of docile. Upon learning this, I entered the quest to clear as much negativity from myself as possible. Things to clear came in the form of indoctrinations, discriminations, thoughts, issues, trauma, anything internal that debilitated me, and made me feel bad about myself, or about others.

My job was to become as light, and as clear minded as I could, – as depicted in Egyptian hieroglyphs, 'As light as the feather of Maat, as it Balances on the Scales'. I then realised why both books were necessary! In fact, I continued to read many many books, with one on astral projection, in a hope that I would then understand how I was doing it. I found that I couldn't do it from the instructions in a book, it just wouldn't work whenever I tried, I guess that's because it had already come natural to me; thus, I was still none the wiser, so continued to have absolutely no control over when it was going to happen to me, which suggests a higher 'Me' is doing it! It still remains a mystery now, – well not so much of a mystery, I just accept it as part of Me and something I do. I also believe, I purposely couldn't do it at my human will, because I'm not supposed to be using it at my own leisure, or for the pleasure of just doing It, like some sort of party trick just because I can. I believe thus far, it has been awakened in me for an ordained divine, very much orchestrated reason. I also believe, had I pushed to do it by the books instructions, I would've been breaking a law in the spirit realm. So, if I had continued, fuck knows where I would've ended up and what could've captured me.

Although the books I have read mildly helped, my process and way to do things all came from me. I began to realise that the books weren't really growing me or unlocking me like I expected. I also already knew a lot of what they were saying, so they just became like confirmation to me instead of new knowledge. They also just seemed to be another place I invested my confidence, rather than look to myself for answers. I was routinely opening a book when I felt confused or had a problem and not really getting to the root, just reliant on the book. They never really explained anything that wasn't surface, and always seemed to come back to, (love thy neighbour as you would want to be loved yourself) not really telling you how to love 'Your-Self', which should've been one of the first things taught! They didn't even say that it is of the upmost importance to love the 'Self' first? Instead a good deed done brings many, which is 'Not' true! As unscrupulous people just end up taking the piss, you will also become in danger of becoming an over giver! The books were always filled with affirmations and rituals that would've had no chance of working, - Because the root of one's issues would still be there, reigning supreme, hidden and left to rise up through the ego, of which was still leading me towards the bad guys, then chastising me when shit went wrong, although it had encouraged me in the first place to go in said direction. Ego being the narcissist that it is! It fought tooth and nail to keep the negative dialogue going, hence the programme running… No! The books just didn't go deep enough, in fact they focused on formalities and fairy tales, which held the ego constructed self in place.

Telling people to become passive, in order to attract their Good and their counterpart, amongst other things - is not it. In fact, the world is full of your counterparts in one-way or another, what you unconsciously believe you are is who you will attract. Everyone you meet is your mirror until you connect with your true essence, – Your-Self.

You have your own power inside of you, it is your right to experience personal empowerment, you do not need another to feel whole. Seduction by romantic illusions that don't exist, likened to the characters in a fairy tale are metaphors, warnings. No one is coming to rescue you, only you can rescue you! You are your knight in shining armour! Although some of you are in couples or seek to be in a union, it must be said that this is a solo journey with regards to your energy, including the upholding of your health, both mentally and spiritually, this is your primary reason for being here. Your physical, the body which is what you need to get about, automatically remains balanced if self- awareness is sought, - what you believe on the inside manifests on the outside. Believing in fairy tales diminishes your power, it not only wastes time, but sets you up to become an enabler. You are unaware that most of the time, you are just attracting what you need to heal within yourself, but cannot see or understand that is what it is. Chances are, you would become an enabler, because you would be accepting treatment that you wouldn't normally accept if you didn't think the person was your divine counterpart, masculine, feminine or whatever the hell they are being called nowadays Twin Flame!

Anyway, it's just another trick of the custodian. The only divine masculine or feminine you need, is the balance of your own male and female divine energy within, after that whatever comes to you is a bonus! Trusting in someone else's intuition, rather than your own, will only lead you into the darkness captive to the matrix.

The matrix is strewn with destructive concepts and principles to lead us as far away from our truth as possible. Many of us have been forced into victimhood, forced into that energy throughout our childhood, in which during that time, an inability to maintain personal boundaries was developed. This made us put our guard down with people that we had no business in trusting, - as a result we were propelled towards a conformist-mindset, prevented from stepping into our own energy, or holding faith in ourselves or our own intuition. This has made us scared of making choices, and trusting in our own inner wisdom, or even hear it. Instead we float around on old stagnant energy, not letting go of people and situations, thus preventing ourselves from truly moving on! The sad thing is, we don't even know we are doing it, because we are programmed to think it normal, it doesn't even occur to us to think things can be, or should be any different. Letting go of the notion of loss is the only way we can transform, courage is needed for this. I also noticed a kind of book author worshiping, likened to how people are with so called famous people, - a transference of 'Will' happens, through association and attention. With that said I put the bloody books down!

I bathed in Himalayan salt and scrubbed myself with lemons, in ancient times they were used to cut through bitterness and cleanse the astral body, it made my skin feel really soft too! I burnt candles and repeated affirmations, I wore various crystals, changed my diet, and died many times metaphorically speaking. I endured so much pain to the point that I thought I was really going to die. I ended up with many diaries, I journaled my life, my fears and any discriminations that came up, I literally took myself apart. Through uncensored automatic writing, I could read back and hear what was really going on in me, what I really thought and believed, I was in conscious contact with my unconscious. I was able to work out who inflicted the most hurt, who continued to do so, and faced them both inside of myself and literally. In my head I would replay conversations I'd had, noticing how they made me feel, if they had triggered me, - what about them triggered me, and how I had reacted, against how I wished I had reacted. I was teaching myself how not to feed into negative energy or thoughts, instead I was analysing why I would be thinking that way… Considering I had already addressed the root, so needed to work out why uninvited thoughts, would continuously come to circle around in my mind, like sharks circling their prey! To later discover that the thought forms are a deliberate feature of the constructed false self, to deliberately keep me in a victim mentality. I quickly realised that my task was to catch them before they grew into an issue within my mind, to prevent myself from falling into the trap of becoming them, this takes immense discipline! Catch them, meaning acknowledge them as being there, then let go. No questions asked - like watching them float past without being tempted to focus on them, stop them, or question them.

Doing that prevents them from solidifying, and growing to further seek company to validate them, in the form of the 'Misery Loves Company Crew'. I was learning how to pay attention to detail, I would walk through shopping centres, (of course when I was shopping) and made a point of noticing things. A bin that might have been a different colour to the rest, did it have anything on top of it? A person that I may have seen earlier walk into the same shop I had gone into, the expression on a child's face, and if they flinched as the person they were with talked to them, or chastised them, smells, – how people walked, did they walk hips thrust forward, which is supposed to mean sex/lust driven, Or did they walk hips pushed back, which would mean the opposite to forward! Did they hold their heads down, any eye contact? because guarantee whoever I had eye contact with, I always saw them again! Did they walk with their shoulders leaning forwards, slightly wrapped? as this is a sign of protecting the heart, or hiding something, or feeling vulnerable. I became conscious of what I was thinking, and made a point of listening to myself, I could hear my constructed thoughts as they traipsed through my mind, so could better understand what got me into certain experiences that would inevitably cause certain outcomes, - I was able to identify the role I was playing, this enabled me to intercept cycles of repetition that would previously put me in environments that I had no business being in. I was seeing how I based everything on physical appearance, how I ignored how they made me feel, which in turn enabled me to become influenced by their energy.

How the intensity of their vibration, teamed with matching hidden desires or requirements had got me caught! From that I began to notice the character I was playing, in unison to the kinds of characters I was attracting. I could see who created the most drama in my life, so I analysed their back story, along with my emotional need that led me to them in the first place, - in a hope that by telling them how their bullshit was affecting me they would stop, or at least validate me (neither happened) so, I either chose to walk away, or if family, forgive through a need to feel loved by them, (which they never did), so I'd go back for more, till I could take no more! Being related through blood on the earth plane is not it, the majority are merely stooges, as 'real' family is in relation to spirit and how we vibrationally match. The ending being, I chose myself and walked away completely, – Never turning back! I had to unlearn society and family ideologies. In 'Divine' timing I stumbled across David Icke's book, 'I Am Free I am Me', the truths it contained, reconfigured the false doctrines that had been placed within my belief system, – it removed the rose- tinted glasses.

We are matched, through our insecurities and fears through issues we refuse to look at. We are connected through similarities, and vibrational alignment. Corresponding unconscious emotions, in relation to what another does not accept about themselves, is what attracts us to each other. Strange as this may sound, people outwardly display what you unconsciously don't accept or like about yourself, that is why (unbeknownst to you) they irritate you, (rub you up the wrong way) because they have triggered the part of you that you are in denial about, that is how mirroring and projecting works. Whenever matching sexual energy is involved, people get emotional triggering mixed up, with what they perceive to be love at first sight. There are no soul mates or twin flames! only kindred Spirits. We have many counterparts pertaining to (Our Parts!) The day you choose to grow out of your issues, is the day your life, relationships, and way of relating change. Few will walk forward with you, others you will leave behind.

The devil, custodian entity feeds on dejection and fear, (the shadow side), that is why it chooses to play games with our mind. Its job is to create insecurities, then prod at them with thought forms to disable us. Leading us into believing we are mere flesh and blood, full of issues and inadequacies. Along with internalizing what is deemed to be fearful, it then uses them to debilitate us. At the same time, it feeds off the light that we subsequently deny exists within us, by turning every hope into a fear. This then blocks us from the 'True Love' we have for ourselves. The custodian knows that once we are in touch with our Love and Light, we are on our way home! Its influence over us will then become almost impossible.

# 𝔓RINCIPLE {13}

I was searching for similarities to my experiences, - my spiritual side, what I knew to be real. I wanted to know about Energy! I didn't really tell anyone what was happening to me, at the same time I had very few people around me that I could trust, therefore, my road became very lonely. Unsure of the final destination, accompanied by a spark inside that wouldn't give up, couldn't give up, every time presenting a positive, to show me that I was on the right path! I then entered the 'Dark Night of the Soul', which was profound more than anything else! One night as I lay in bed wide awake in the early hours, I took me to a place within, where I learnt what Ego was and was not.

The place I thought was inside of me, where I would normally hear instruction, advice, repeatedly chastise myself, judge others, fear consequence, assume, pick situations and people that were not good for me was gone, - went quiet, – had pissed off. I begged for help to hear something, anything! When I asked for it to tell me what was going on - to explain, it was silent? Nothing! No answers for me, as if it had come to the end of the line. Like it couldn't go any further with me, because its basis was untruth, so was incapable of transmitting truth, because all along it was a Programme, - A fucking PROGRAMME! the Game! designed to hide who and what we really are. At that moment my perception of myself and everything took on a whole new view, it was the strangest thing to both witness and experience. At that moment I was again like a fly on the wall in my own life, - as the observer. I truly felt alone in the light of the dark, in silence, wide awake with myself. I questioned if I was dead, or going to die! Then the moment I let go of questioning and accepted what was happening, was the moment I realised that the voice was not only a programme, and that it wasn't real, but also that it was a construct that lived outside of me. I then felt at peace, joyous in my realisation, like I had always known, but just needed to get out of my own way.

The journey is both treacherous and magical. I had gone too far to turn back, although turning back was never an option! I had gone so far that anything less than wonder and growth wouldn't do, the trust in my intuition my higher self, had been fuelled with every step, in return I was being fed and built. Gradually I could finally hear Me, I could finally differentiate between Self, and the dialogue and emotion coming in from outside of me, I was no longer wearing the coat, or cloaked in the deceit of the ego - the matrix! My search of clear, is, and was, relentless to say the least. I became able to detect if someone had negative vibes or placed a negative vibe/emotion onto me, I even kind of stopped physically ageing as a result. I could tell what energy was mine and what projections belonged to someone else, whereas before I was a carrier and receiver of everything, and slowly dying under the weight. I learnt that whomever we have a connection with has a potential opportunity to attach themselves, harness and syphon energy from us through playing control games. I also learnt that whoever we have a connection with, is here for us to possibly learn a lesson about ourselves from, and them from us. I learnt that the ego false constructed self constantly looks for external things to attach to, in order to assure its longevity. The ego needs to be validated by other egos, as in people, to thrive, – hence the comradery when the misery loves company gang, or self-righteous gang, amongst other non-productive attitudes are at play, all sharing similarities to make their internal reality feel whole.

The false self can only exist when it is given attention, whether good or bad! Its only purpose is to keep you asleep within the confines of the constructed mind, - the matrix. The false self feeds off the fear that it provides. The pain we feel when a connection doesn't turn out, is created by originally listening to the voice of the ego false self, and following it. It is responsible for initially leading us, and encouraging us to invest our energy with trust and hope. We only experience pain through, and because of the false self, other than that, pain does not exist in the non-physical realm. When you are attached to anything but yourself, you will remain in an undercurrent of physical pain and longing. You will seek to have control over the thing you are attached to, in a hope of reducing feelings of inevitable pain, – not realizing, that you are only building on it with your investment of the control you seek to have over it, thus enhancing its eventual intensity, upon you feeling false abandonment. I say 'false', because you're not really being abandoned, you would only really be abandoned if 'Your Self' abandons you! You need to let go of control in order to be your authentic self.

Demonic egos have a way of knowing what hidden fears we harbour, they know what we are not sure about, and what strengths we are still trying to integrate within. Their job is to prod at us, to aggravate us, in order to disarm us, - then coax us into submitting to their needs, (the way of the Narcissist). Just remember! Custodian entity 'Success', is always subject to your lack of self-worth. It is a test of how much you will tolerate and for how long! You must take responsibility for your own fears and issues, as in the need for validation, financial, companionship or whatever else your false self deems them a knight in shining armour for! When you are in an ego-based relationship, or situation- ship, it will always eventually hurt, because you are constantly being made to use your energy to stroke their personality, thus, fuel their false self. You will also be automatically driven into becoming 'your' false self! You will not get anything in return but hurt and confusion, uncertainty and disregard, distrust, false love & care - if any care at all! You will then be led into situations that cause more pain, not love! True Love is Self-validation. Attachments attained for the specific purpose of making you feel as if you exist, that you are worthy, accepted or deserving, – in other words to replace what you think you are lacking, will control you, and put you in a needy mind set! It is not our responsibility to rescue others, especially when it's to our own detriment! You will become drained when your energy is being taken, harnessed and harvested by another.

'Lack' keeps us tied to the ego false self! The notion of not having enough or not being enough is dominated by the false self, the notion of needing to give up on yourself, in order to survive is ego false-self based. Realise that you are being tricked, you need to give up your false self in order to survive! Not the other way around!

Detach from limiting beliefs when needy people show up in your life, - you will then see that it is only validation they want from you! You must 'Not' provide it or else you Will be devaluing yourself and your boundaries. You must realise that colluding with the false self, believing that you are the ego self, is part of the construct, specifically designed to destabilise you. The closer you get to your authentic self, the more you get to 'value' yourself. The more you value yourself, the more you stop validating any Ego. The less you validate the ego, the less you require exterior validation! No longer be prepared to take those risks with yourself, as it is a form of crazy, - part of the programming!

# 𝔓RINCIPLE {14}

The closer I got to 'My Self' by the relinquishing of the programmed self, the closer the parallel planes of existence came. Although they had always been there, - the vibration I was on had not permitted me to embrace them fully in their totality. – Instead they seemed to randomly privilege me with their presence, by voluntarily showing me stuff, whilst at the same time mindful of not scaring the shit out of me. To be honest, I did actually ask for them not to ever do, or show me anything that will freak me out, they have continued to respect my request.

I have never seen anything that I can't handle. Everything that came before, however random, prepared me to accept whatever was to come next, and nothing has ever harmed me, and to be honest no-thing would've been allowed to. Everything that has happened to me has been deliberate.

There are no coincidences, I had no choice than to surrender to acknowledging, and I am glad that I did, it has been an honour to assist and become. I feel very 'Very' privileged.
I had decided to cut my grass, so I opened my small brick shed, which stood just outside to the left of my front door. My attention was instantly drawn to some withered and dead crispy dry ivy, that had grown through the corner of the shed roof. I then had a passing thought, 'I wonder what it would be like if they grew?' I don't know why. At the same time, I kind of thought nothing of it, and continued to take the lawn mower out. I spent over two hours cutting my lawn and preening my garden. So, when it was time to put the mower back, - to my amazement when I opened the shed door, there in front of me, draped through the ceiling was a long cluster of fully grown, brand new in appearance, shiny green ivy! with leaves that looked almost plastic because they were so fresh and new, just born, it was unbelievable! The fresh ivy leaves stayed until they withered away, through lack of sunlight, I guess, as there was only darkness in the shed because the door to it was always closed and locked. Although, one would question how they got there in the first place, to grow full form in two hours, - considering it being dark, and plant life needing full photosynthesis to grow as beautifully as they did. I think it had something to do with my question, or, did my thought manifest the ivy? That would mean that my question wasn't in fact a question then? I actually think I was being told what was going to happen, and just translated it as a question to myself! Who knows? just like what came first the chicken or the egg! 'Ha-ha!' either way it was a manifestation.

The same day, I had decided to wear a pair of jeans that were hanging over the banister upstairs. As I was about to pick them up, I noticed a fairly large grass stain on the back, - they were a clean pair of jeans! They had been hanging over the banister because I had put them there to dry, fresh from taking them out of the washing machine the day before. I had absolutely no idea how the grass stain got there, and I couldn't recall doing it because I hadn't. I just thought it strange and accepted that I would have to find a different pair to wear, and walked into my bathroom to shower. When I came out I glanced at the jeans as I walked past, to see that the stain had completely gone, disappeared, vanished! I held the jeans in my hands feeling dumbfounded.

I have seen the grid that surrounds this planet. The best way to describe it is likened to white fluorescent tubes like the ones on a neon sign. The grid forms a crisscross pattern above us, surrounding this planet like a dome.

I once saw a female in form, a woman with blond hair, with jet black eyes, – not just the pupils the whole eye! It knew that I could see it and became scared, I felt its energy and just walked past it, continuing my day - thinking what the fuck! But chuffed at the same time! couldn't wait to tell someone about that one. I have seen people and vehicles disappear, strange thing about them is they seemed to always want me to see them, and then disappear just so I could see that too!

The times I would be walking along the road side pavement, and for no reason my leg would start to hurt, then I would notice ahead of me, or on the other side of the road at some distance, a person. As they got closer I could tell from how they walked that something was wrong with their leg, the same leg that was hurting me, - then as I got past them the pain would stop. I was also able to feel another's pain without them physically displaying it, along with their sadness and emotions without them telling me about it. I found that when I acknowledged to myself that neither pain or emotion was mine, and or where it was coming from, whatever I was feeling would disappear. Sometimes as I walked, I would sense the person walking behind me, then would wander if they were male or female, and what colours they were wearing, then turn around and see them as just so...

The spider that walked across my front room floor, then disappeared in front of me, in a small spark of blue-white light, as it crossed into another dimension.

The evening I sat on my sofa and the room turned red, 'Everything' turned red, all other colour taken out leaving just red! like when you look through a piece of clear red - cellophane gift wrap or sweetie paper - RED. At the same time my white cat had formed a 10-inch primary blue block of colour around its body, chances are it had always surrounded it, but I just couldn't see it until then.

The whole experience lasted for what felt like ages. I remember blinking frantically in a hope of seeing things turn back to normal, thinking it was my eyes but it wasn't. You can imagine I was both relieved and grateful when full colour was restored. Again, it was something I was meant to see, something I was being shown.

Another time, I lay on my sofa with my eyes closed, to suddenly see a dazzling bright light shining. My eyes where closed so thought how could this be. Slightly stunned and a tad scared, I opened one eye, to see if it was the lamp that sat in the corner, reflecting back at me through my eyelids, – the lamp wasn't switched on. The light was shining from inside of me, in my head, it was brighter than the bulb in the lamp, - it also had a slight orange hue to it, likened to the sun, instead of yellowy like a light bulb.

Every time I read this bit back to myself, I feel uncomfortable, - I guess I'm not sure whether to leave it in, anyway here goes! I have also seen a big dragon flying through the sky, sounding a tad profound I know! However, it was obviously through a dimensional tear. I'll tell you about that some other time… Maybe!

As I lay in bed sensing a presence in my room, I chose to turn over and ignore it. The instant I closed my eyes, I came out of my body and went through the top right corner of my bedroom wall. Instead of going outside, I found myself going at a tremendous speed through what I now know to be worm holes. At first, I felt scared because of the speediness, then as I rocketed through, whilst bending and sharp turning, I began to feel erotic sexual energy, so began to like it, "I say with a big smile!" This enabled me to let go of the fear, at the same time gaining access to my peripheral vision, where I could see colours blurring and blending into each other, tailing off with the speed at which I was traveling past. My destination is vague, although I had two entities at each side of me, guiding me through and protecting me. I didn't look at what they looked like I just knew they were there. I also don't think the place we were going through was very nice, a lower plane of existence with entities trying to grab at me, I was assured my protectors wouldn't let go of me, or let me 'get got'. This form of traveling happened quite a few times. At first the two were accompanying me, then I would be doing it on my own, or so they had me think, as I would only sense their presence in my bedroom, not whilst I travelled. I also began to really like it, and looked forward to going to bed, with a hope that I would go traveling, as so to experience the erotic ascent, I loved it! I would go to different dimensions, jump from roof top to roof top, sit in the branches of tall trees and watch people going by beneath.

Sometimes I transported to what seemed like random houses and centers/shopping malls, and move things or touch the people there. A few times I was chased by rowdy people who could see me, like the movie Inception; I guess I was somewhere I wasn't supposed to be, this would sometimes knock me back into my body. Other than that, I was able to escape them by ascending upwards at a rapid speed, however, this wouldn't always work due to exhaustion. I think not having harvested enough life force on the physical plane, resulted in not being able to summon enough energy to elevate, so instead, 'being knocked back in', I think with the help of my guides, through what I can only describe as abruptly landing back into my physical body! immediately opening my eyes, assuring myself that I was back on this plane. Knowing that we occupy multiple dimensions, I'm not sure what form of me they were seeing? Other times I would nearly become trapped, as other world entities and aggressive types would be able to sense me and chase me, attempting to block the windows and doorways out, which were down to my perception, because they were really portals. I never became trapped, because I didn't belong there so it wasn't permitted. As the student, I began to realise that those realms had no power over my life force or me, I would always be able to escape, or bring 'Myself' back to my body and this reality in an instant, – although an invisible protection always remained at my side. I realised that some could see me, especially children, and others would experience me as a ghost.

# Principle {15}

There have been a couple of times when I was out of my body for too long. One particular parallel dimension I found myself in, I saw something that made me feel very uncomfortable, so had to stop myself from getting involved in the narrative! I remained as the observer, to protect my consciousness from becoming enmeshed within a dimension that, I guess I had clearly outgrown at some point in time. However, at that point wherever I was, became all too real, which made me become worried that I couldn't get back to this dimension. Then a thought that I was to listen for my heartbeat, and my breathing came to me, and as soon as I did this I was back. I must say it felt like a close shave. I really thought I was going to be stuck on another alternative timeline, and was going to leave my two daughters here without a mother. In theory it would have been just my physical body, - as my consciousness was at the time occupying another.

Strange, on that timeline I was standing in a small kitchen with someone who I recall asking what I looked like, and was told that I looked like myself? The person obviously saw me as the body that I was in. I didn't ask any more questions; however, the whole experience further demonstrates, that a version of me, may have had access to the physical body on this dimension whilst I was out of it. Or maybe me jumping into their body, cancelled them out into a trance like kind of state for the duration of me being in it? To be honest I didn't want to find out, I came back to my body as soon as I sensed my heart beat and felt my breathing, so was never really unattached or vacant for the taking.

Another time I was woken out of my sleep, to feel the bottoms of my feet hurting, to then see at the foot of my bed, loads of people filling my room, just standing there looking at me, they were not as solid as the entity in the hat, but a little less dense but all focused on me. The energy coming from them is what made my feet hurt, I guess to deliberately wake me up. I didn't even ask them what they wanted, – I felt no fear just protected by them, then I just turned, closed my eyes and went back to sleep. At times like that I astound myself with my ability to refuse to converse. I can only think that at the time, it was because I wasn't impressed with being woken by them, or woken up in that way. I actually don't have an answer, it was just another what the fuck moment! Anyway, like I said, I have had a lot of experiences likened to what I have already told you. Again, I will also say that I feel privileged to have been chosen to experience them.

The purpose for me mentioning otherworld happenings, is to further acquaint you with the existence of other energies, timelines, and dimensions that reside parallel to us. I believe, so as not to scare me, the ones in my bedroom at the foot of my bed that night, appeared to resemble human form, did so, so I could feel some sort of familiarity and likeness in form akin to mine, other than show up as energy formations, – which is what we really are. On entry the soul/consciousness takes on the physical appearance of a body, along with its compression. Because of this casing we associate with it more than our soul, believing it is what we are, we then become attached to the human brain as the reference for our reality as it operates the body. The ego false self is then born. The human brain processes things attuned to what the ego-false self sees and understands, being; what it is familiar with, and what emotions it creates to go with it. I believe the ones in my bedroom were trapped life force, ancestral energy even! - from one or many of the other timeline dimensions, as we occupy many, wanting to go 'Home'.

The two little imp girls peering through my front room window one day... I call them imps because I don't know what other descriptive name to give to them. They weren't tall, and had slightly bulbous features, they were not of our earth plane, or dimension and certainly weren't dead people running around. I sat up on my sofa and saw them just peering in at me. Their skin was a slightly grey - off white in colour, with scraggly dark hair, big pointed top ears and thick eye brows with normal looking hands - They just looked very nosey and inquisitive. When they saw that I saw them, they weren't there anymore.

I was standing looking out of my bedroom window, then turned to glimpse a light brown and white mouse on my bed, between my pillows. Horrified I ran out of my room closing the bedroom door behind me. Being squeamish, I ran to my next-door neighbor, and got her to go into my bedroom to help get the mouse out, but there was no mouse, and no hole anywhere for any mouse to run into, or out, nothing, no sign! We never found it... It had disappeared! and my neighbour just thought I had nothing better to do, although she did take it as an opportunity to have a nose around my bedroom. I had to put that bit in, she has since passed, so want her to know that I know! Ha ha!

My daughter Rochelle, who is now grown, has given me her permission to share the day when she found a photograph, on her then blackberry mobile phone, that she didn't take. At first look, the photo appeared to be of her, eyes closed suspended in the air, with white light that looks like energy trailing from her body, or, to her body. I then had the idea of transferring the photo to the laptop so that we could see it on a bigger screen, and take another photo of it with my mobile phone, but this time with the flash from my phone switched on, as if to be looking into the dark of the picture. However, upon further inspection of the second photo that I had captured, nothing could've prepared us for what we saw next! In the photo, directly behind her, and standing, was a tall figure with the corners of its mouth turned down, and eyes closed, receiving her energy or vice versa? Within the figure we could see a number of people, spirits both young and old, which appeared to change facial expression the more we looked. Animals and shadow entities with cat eyes began looking back at us, - even today the picture is still live! Friends who have looked at the picture, not only see what we see, albeit sometimes slightly different, point out things within the picture that we hadn't seen. Anyway, within an hour of finding the photo the phone rang. When answered, all we could hear was high pitched sounds and noises, echoes, and vague but faint audible scrambled voices at the other end, It felt as if it was some sort of otherworld communication. It was really intriguing to say the least! Some years later, I kind of managed to work out what the live photo was trying to tell us.

However, how it was taken or rather appeared on my daughter's phone remains a mystery (sort of). Maybe one day someone will be able to shed some light on it, no doubt they wanted us to find it. Looking at the time stamp on the phone, - it was taken middle of the day, at the time when my daughter was sitting in her car very much awake. The background to the photo looked very similar to my front room doorway?

Rogue spirits, are disembodied spirits that have attached themselves to a place, or habit in a person. The habit-based ones are called entities. Through not having the use of a physical body. In order to feel, they attach to a human body that has a habit suited to their own otherwise starved desire. For the human occupied by the entity, the habit becomes an addiction, that becomes difficult to drop, as the need for it to be experienced is increased by the added weight and magnified desires of the entity who needs to feed. This feed is accessed through the shadow body that resides within the outer energy body of the human vessel, - the aura. Temptation is encouraged, and engaged through the entities hunger, deriving from a need to cover up a truth that would inevitably set the host free. An inability to face one's weaknesses, a truth or loss of memory developed through trauma of a significant occurrence, at some point along your journey through lives - will hamper you for life. The trauma can be understood as something that has been transformed into a lack, pertaining to a subtle but effective drainage to your life force, this creates a gap for the entity to attach.

A gap that you will always seek to fill until healed. The entity creates a kind of PTSD by making you relive trauma, over and over again, through eliciting visions, feelings, or both to enhance the intensity of the occurrences within you. This prevents you from ever growing or detecting what is really happening to you. The entity feeds from the intensity of the occurrence, whilst at the same time using it as a way to block awareness, causing the host to perpetually run from what needs to be healed. The only way to get rid of the addiction entity is to get rid of the need, – in order to get rid of the need, one would need to face the root of the trauma, the 'Without', that created it, and feel the pain/emotion attached. So, the entity aids in creating an addiction in the person, in order to feed, to stay alive, and in control. We choose to call the rest of the rogue spirits and imprints ghosts. Some haunt us, leaving us to rationalise the experiences, resulting in denial that they are there.

I had to deal with one for my youngest daughter, I think she was about 7 at the time. 'He', a Georgian looking, grey complexioned spirit, complete with fancy nobleman suit, white powdered girly wig, frilly cuffed shirt and breeches, not forgetting his long socks. Liked to scare Molly by standing in her energy field. I don't know how but I just knew what to do. We first created a ritual with glitter, that was to give Molly a sense of control over its banishment, we then recited some words together as we threw the glitter out of the front door.

Her, being a little girl, I knew its banishment had to seem magical, hence, the glitter. In Molly's mind the spirit was being thrown out with it! I then went into my bedroom, and took myself into Molly's energy vibration, located the spirit and banished it. I watched as it glided past me towards my window, it then turned and looked at me, laughing before it left through the wall of my then bedroom. It had a stupid kind of face, – its mouth sort of went from ear to ear, it also wore lipstick and had white powder on its face.

One Saturday evening, I lay on my bed horizontally after having a bath, to see materialise in front of me. A figure with a long 2ft beak with short smooth hair on it. No hair on his head, he had beautiful piercing eyes with thick eyebrows, a beautiful muscular human body, not too bulky, my preference ha ha, with soft smooth skin. He didn't speak. He then leant forward towards me and I said, 'Human Please'. I have no recollection of what happened after that, just a blankness. I can tell you that, although it may come across as strange to you, I had no fear, none whatsoever because I know him. I welcomed him and acknowledged in the moment, that he must have needed to connect with me. I call him beaky for obvious reasons. With almost all who have visited me, my vibration naturally adjusts to accommodate them, or they adjust it for me. With a trusting sense of home, and familiarity I accept. With beaky, I was left with a longing to see him again, which lasted a few days.

There was a time when spirits would come to me, and I would send them back towards a light, that I now call the light of attachment and return. I've now since realised that sending them towards the light is sending them back here or to a parallel dimension.

We don't actually die; our souls consciousness is eternal. The tunnel I had found myself in, on the conveyer belt with the lights at the end confirms that. Although the reason for the return is double ended, it is primarily because they haven't completed their journey to warrant going home. So, basically this shitty planet 'earth', and lower vibrational existence, will go on for as long as it takes until you decide to wake up. I also realise that by sending them back, I was kind of aiding the custodian. However, I have great faith, that who or whatever I was sending towards the lights, has a full unconscious intention of eventually desiring to go home. Although they had chosen to choose the light of attachment, at the time there would've been no other option for them, because they wouldn't be energetically unattached from this dimension enough, or vibrationally high enough to do otherwise in their current state of mind or being. Anyway, it's better than having them roam about disembodied scaring and pissing people off.

With that said, I have two jobs; to lead the people who are ready, 'Home', by sharing the process. And, before I knew what I know now! To guide them back when they were not ready. So, in actual fact the custodian serves a purpose, although it instigated the problem! which is, to disengage people from the source 'Self', by inner- pressing them with the false constructed Ego-self! in order to discourage them from looking for it, or even realise it exists.

It is for you to then tap into your recollection of the Infinite Creator, to become awakened within, in order for you to become aware of not belonging here, thus want to search for the truth in order for you to go home! However, the only way for you to do this, is to acknowledge that you have been programmed, and exist within an illusion controlled by a disembodied, custodian entity constructed matrix.

# Principle {16}

All that I have experienced in the form of scary, have been like doorways that needed to be walked through, in order to understand that there is nothing to fear as we all contain the same creative energy. That any occupants on the other side, are just vibrations from different lives and factions, that have been used as blocks to our perception, meaning... They are us! We manifested some through our shadow side, disgraced, and perceived as ugly in form, due to the dismissive emotions we attached. Someone's vivid recollection knows exactly what they are, because the images have been used to play characters in horror movies, but only in order to plant a certain visual perception into us to intensify fear, and fear of them. Planting this further creates distance between the self.

The movies depict what we are, they also subliminally command what we are to reject, attack, repel, fear, and what to use to hurt others, when really is all they are; is expressions of us that we have created to free ourselves from the energies they hold. However, in order to really free ourselves from them, they are to be understood and accepted. They are our symbol of balance because they are our shadow. We actually created them through energy that we dispensed and dismissed! Likened to the narcissist, that would seem to have no soul and can only stay functional through the energy of attention we give it. It has no power without your reflection, however, the shadow operates in the opposite way, existing through the attention we don't give it! Like the child or pet that we choose to ignore becomes unruly, – sighting that even negative attention is better than none! Its task is to become noticed, light needs to be shone onto it… To ignore it, is a form of negative non-attention. And so, because it already exists, the shadow side manifests outwardly in others and in films, – as what is perceived ugly, the badness in us that we would never consider owning or acting out, treating it like a child born with abnormalities, given birth to in the olden days, that is subsequently hidden away because the parents are ashamed of it, although it is the result of the parents genes! (sorry I didn't know how else to example the depth of my point). Whilst experiencing fear and trauma, we unknowingly created those shadows, to inhibit ourselves to further solidify the belief in fear, the matrix, however, before that they didn't exist.

We manifested them through the attention we gave to fear, yes, we actually gave them the energy to exist, - then started to unconsciously project the same fear into what we thought was an abyss, (actually we didn't think at all) to subsequently return to us, then onto each other in every way imaginable, some embrace their fears and act them out, the majority choose to not! We chose to nurture each other's projections by relating them into becoming real! Which ensured a continuous rotation of thought, and fear that nobody wanted to own, that ended up subsequently following us.

Belief in your higher energy, pertaining to the ultimate Infinite Creator of All, is what will keep you on the right path, it is our 'Code!' I am saying that there are rules pertaining to morals and integrity, - dark energy and good energy, – positive energy, and negative energy, it is the language that is used here, but does not exist where we come from, because there our energy is already purified. The way 'Home' has been disguised, just not in the way we thought.

"We Do Not Originally Come from Here!" Shocking as it may seem... We Don't! Nothing is as it seems, everything is opposite to the way it really is... Everything is an illusion. In reality we all occupy the same space on many planes of existence and timelines, that run concurrently to ours on different vibrations, whilst at the same time belonging to different factions and realms of reality, which again could be many... Seriously!

My task here is to uncover what enables us to ignore the signs that encourage us to believe we are merely human, physical, when we are really spirit housed in a physical vessel! Consciousness inside body suit, – that unconsciously existed within multiple lives, manifested attachments that now need to be lived through, until we realise that they are not real, thus releasing attachment to them! Each emotion traumatic or otherwise, has to go back to where it was issued and generated - in order for you to be free of it. It is like you have become responsible for something that wasn't yours, and wasn't real, but chose to carry it anyway. Because you carried it you grew a relationship to it... You are believing it to be yours, and because of that you believe it is how you really feel; however, we have to pay for all the shit we bring into the dimensions, nothing gets cancelled out! Growth must be made towards realisation of the self, - until this is done you are guaranteed to come back over and over again.

To enable you to go home to the source of all infinite creation... Home, you must release yourself from all your emotional attachments on the parallel dimensions, by realising the emotions attached to them here, (face your ways) they are not set in stone! Know that the energy trauma follows you until purified. So called Déjà vu, is not your imagination playing tricks to be brushed aside, it is trying to jog your memory, to wake you up. Just like being followed into this life by past life entity's, and vibrations we knew before! albeit in different disguises, parading as family members and so-called soul mates.

In books they are depicted romantically as your other half, or as beings of good, when really, they have come to assist you to rectify shit you created. Because you are unaware of this, they instead through your connection to them, prevent and dismantle what you try to create in this life, whether for good or bad! most times to prevent you remembering, and to ensure longevity for the energy they bring..., either way this is not to be taken lightly folks!

Forgive yourself! Any action done against your physical body is 'not' what is important, how you were left feeling is what holds the gems! Partly because, feelings are unfamiliar to our natural make up, they are entities in the spiritual realm, each one is like a dead weight, – you must release every emotion, they do not belong to you! Forgiving yourself and the other person or situation, is for you, not them, it releases the energetic trigger and attachment we have to it. Every feeling and emotion resides in the external energy body, when triggered, we take that emotion and project how it makes us feel onto another, and hold them accountable for it whether good or bad.

Most emotional responses are created for us during childhood, (like when a child falls we run to comfort them, caution them to be careful before they show any emotion) they may not even be hurt, - thus teaching them that to be scared, or whatever emotion the carer is projecting, is what is to be felt when that thing happens to them - god forbid if they have a smothering parent, (this is how bloody hypochondriacs are created). We are also teaching the child what emotion secures what attention. By the time we are adults, we have learnt many ways in which to react, in the form of learnt emotions or learnt behaviours. Whether they become ingrained, to later be used as a crutch to aid the needy in the manipulation and drainage of others, is down to us, and how awake we are! Also, I'm 'Not' saying ignore your children! I'm saying assess if there is damage first before you go projecting your learned emotions on to the child. Compassion without cautionary projections! prevents a child from creating prolonged issues within, pertaining to the incident. Never go to a child when you are being consumed by your own fear!

# Principle {17}

As a person, as people, when we don't know who we are, or what we are, we give our power and ownership of ourselves to others, for a fact, to governments! By giving yourself away, you became disassociated and lost touch with your essence. You went into survival mode. Result being, you no longer felt secure, - thus your fear of bad things happening became amplified! Unknown to you, you had become vulnerable through the loss of connection to your higher self, leaving you to believe you are the physical body and feel unprotected. You then enlisted the responsibility of your protection to police law enforcement; The result being, - mass vulnerability encourages a flawed integrity. People then take advantage of each other, due to our second sight being removed.

Through dilution of the connection with self, we can then no longer spiritually see or sense danger coming, or the intent of what approaches, because we take everything on face (physical) value, rather than through our own true senses. Now in repression, like motherless children we seek acceptance, thus shrink, already been swallowed by becoming brainwashed with one of many 'religions!' Result being, - the people need something to believe in, estranged from self, they are unaware the self exists, - thrown head first from the womb into another's construction of morals, strewn with ideologies with notions that pertain to deservedness, and how to gain external approval on our exterior! and acceptance from a seeming to be 'unforgiving' lord god! We fully turn away from ourselves, we allow full distance! We then choose to invest our energy outside, in people who we believe to not only know better than us, but who we also perceive to be 'Better than us', who teach us that amassing things will make us feel good, make us feel worthy, albeit temporarily! We are unaware that by giving over ourselves to this false ideological mindset, we are in fact giving ourselves over to entity-controlled beings, who are draining and harvesting our life force to secure longevity and control over our soul. Your fear, sorrow, and lack of self-awareness is their pleasure, 'their food'. Can you see it? You help the custodian through the fear that has been instilled in you, you affirm this with your loyalty to religious doctrines, distracted by your dissatisfaction with the societal position bestowed upon you, (the fodder).

Albeit restrictive you accept it. Your lack of self-worth deems you grateful, grateful like a charity, to the point where you will kill each other in order to keep it, thus, remain in sacrifice to it, your souls caught up in a belief system. Becoming so fixated and loyal to it, just because it was passed down to you through generations as far back as you dare to remember. If not obeyed, you would believe yourselves to be sinners! Religion has been used as the scapegoat, to put people in sacrifice to a custodian entity hungry for power! In reference to the bible; Another man's murder does Not absolve you of your so-called sin! There is 'No Sin', only Attachments! and Free will. Attachment being; the unconscious hunger to replicate the intensity of your Souls first ever encumbering chains, thus an anchor to your physical body, - whatever that may look like, whether good or bad. This is how you assist the custodian with trapping your soul to the physical dimension. No one else but You, are responsible for the absolving of these Attachments! However, as you choose to overlook, you are a lamb repeatedly being slaughtered. Sorry! but I'm not here to pacify your personalities, I'm here to tell you how it is! You are Brainwashed, by your inflexibility and inability to see above what you have been fed, your false ego pride won't allow you to question it, or let go to release it in order to clear your perceptions of all the clutter and conditioning. It is vital that you create a clean slate in which you can connect to self, 'Your-self'. Everyone is a victim of these false truths, elicited and controlled by the custodian entity. There is also No Heaven or Hell, Just the alternative dimensions we end up on, in relation to the vibrational frequency's we have become. Our being transposed to other dimensions, is subject to, and set by the attachments we hold, Just like here; 'Until we realise that none of it is real'.

We have been bamboozled, and hoodwinked, put under a spell! We must become masters of our own journey! not a slave to our distractions. Remember! Your life force is your currency - your power! We do not die. You are fulfilling scriptures that were written by man to feed an entity. I will even go as far to say, the nature of the 'Beast Mentality'. It's existence on earth has all been about maintaining a position of power at all costs! Think about it; multitudes of men, women, and children have, and continue to be murdered on so-called religious grounds on a regular basis, for whatever reason, in one way or another. Wars are created specifically to cull large segments of a population (spirit housed in physical body), their energy of terror and fear, syphoned, in order to top up the stocks of the custodian entity life force, to be stored in another realm, like a farmer stores grain! Animals slaughtered, aware of their fate, for people to then consume the flesh. Are you aware, that through their flesh and blood you are also consuming and digesting the animals pain and terror! All around the world, conditioned through religion, you actually take sides! manipulated, into believing you have the right to choose who you think deserves to die, as a consequence for what religion or doctrine they believe they are! Fucked up mindsets! without thought for where these mindsets, or beliefs originally came from, or even what they have to do with you? Yes, things have been written in the bible, as well as other so-called holy scriptures, however, -

God The Most High, does not turn up at a man-made church, with a (most of the time) corrupt preacher or pope parading as the go between! There is 'No' go between, – just You, and Them! The Creators vibration is within you! You are your church! 'Surely' you need to consider why these doctrines have worldwide popularity, and who or what put them there? You are caught up with the colour of each other's skin, race, and cast! to the point where factions have been created, land, air and water brought and owned! as if any of it can really be owned! 'But', you believe it... Whole country's divided, whilst sighting so called royalty as the cream! and most deserving of all... But why? Why, are you so heavily invested in difference when we are all the same? 'Spirit has no colour!' We are all consciousness – 'Energy'. You have blindly gone along with another's set of regulations, again I will say - like a lamb to the slaughter! Can you see what has happened to us as a result of becoming docile? And believing we are a physical body. We are all slaves, slaves captured on this dimension! Your attachment to your beliefs is being used, to not only inflict fear and distance between self but with each-other, as well as manifest pain, to a high degree to provide maximum harvest for the custodian to reap! It doesn't care about you! It only cares about the power in you! It is a carnal energy of low vibration that holds multitudes of souls, Your lifeforce! through influence, spells, sorcery, trickery and deception! You are trapped in a delusion; none of these ideals really matter! In fact, they have 'nothing' to do with you!

When I looked down at myself, my hand looked like a cluster of atoms, still outlined in the shape of a human hand, but made up of fizzy shiny particles, vibrating, light grey and white, bouncing in and out of each other. I wasn't a solid block of colour, I was moving fizzy atoms. Fizzy like white noise on an untuned tv channel, but more defined, loads of molecules moving.

The body we are in is not solid, – how we see ourselves and the things surrounding us, all depend on the vibration we reside on. My body sat upright on the floor whilst I towered above it. Although in the same room with myself, I felt coaxed toward another dimension that felt more like reality… 'Real Home,' realer than here. Comforted that if I was to leave now, it would be the right decision. My only reservation was that my daughters wouldn't be able to get into the house, because I had locked the front door from inside. I then found myself operating my body whilst being outside of it. My consciousness moved my body parts in order for it to go to the door, heavy but doable, I watched my body crawl to my front door and unlock it. I then crawled back after having completed the task; at that point, partially back in my body, I slumped on the floor with my back against my sofa. Prevented by my attachments, obviously, the moment had passed for me to go wherever I thought I was going, 'Home', to wake hours later, finding myself in the same spot in the same position with consciousness integrated… 'I obviously wasn't going to get out of here that easily 'Ha ha'

Transfiguration; I once went to see a medium. As she began speaking to me, I saw a transparent vale drop over her face with my deceased aunty Sandra's face presenting over hers, I just looked in amazement. Years later, as I spoke to a friend in my kitchen, her temperament changed towards me, she switched and became uncharacteristically different, strange? I noticed this and began to feel slightly threatened by her tone and demeaner, (danger of being spiritually attacked) registered within me, at that point I then felt slightly different! She then told me there and then, that my face had changed into a version of me but as a man! I guess whatever transposed over me came to protect me, warding her off by presenting me as a male... Although I recall feeling overcome by a slightly different energy, I felt no sensations to my face. At the same time, I asked her what the fuck she was playing at, she then said she didn't know how to control it (I never asked her what 'it' was) I just assumed she was talking about her energy. In hindsight however, I now realise that she had an entity attachment that wanted to attack me. I wish I had asked her to take a photo of me!

Bilocation; Years ago, A friend and her boyfriend came over one evening for me to cut his hair. He took his t-shirt off in order for me to put a towel around his neck. At first, I saw nothing on his back, then a large tattoo of a coiled snake suddenly appeared, not lifelike, just a drawing of a snake. I said nothing and continued to cut his hair. When it was time for them to leave, – he walked out first, leaving her sitting on the sofa, which I did think strange, but thought nothing of it. I then heard the door nock thinking it was him, when I opened it She was standing outside, she came in, kind of gliding past me... confused! I walked into my front room where I had left her, she was still sitting in the same spot.

She then got up like normal, said her goodbyes and I saw her to the door, I watched her walk down the path then closed the door behind her. Because what happened bothered me immensely, I called her the next day and told her what I had seen, that I had seen her in two places at once and about the snake. I was even more shocked when she didn't seem to be bothered or surprised by what I had said, or even concerned that her spirit had split from her body! That night when I lay down to go to sleep I heard bottles being knocked over outside my front door, and saw a black dog running up my stairs in my peripheral vision, then felt something sit at the bottom of my bed. I wasn't scared just shaken a bit, but knew it had something to do with them. I then found out that both of them were practicing witches, they were into dark arts. I promptly ended any further contact or communication with them.

Over the years my sleeping patterns have changed, meaning, I don't seem to need much sleep anymore, – not that I ever slept deeply in the first place. However, I am now used to functioning on about 4 hours of sleep or less. At first, I thought this was strange and believed that I had insomnia, but after realising that I still felt rested when I woke up, regardless of how little sleep I'd had, I decided to accept it as just another 'Sharon-ism'. With that said, over the last few years or so, since the beginning of writing this book, I have been waking up feeling as if I've been fighting a battle, feeling slightly drained, my body aching, stiff and feeling heavy. At times being woken to hear talking in my ear, sometimes saying negative things, or in a language that I don't understand.

Or I would be astral traveling to places, being tracked and followed by people I knew to be dead, or - encountering people I no longer spoke to, - coming to me, saying things that were not true, as if trying to plant false bullshit into my thoughts, or trying to entice me to eat food or drink from them, (eating food is a No no when visiting other dimensions) –all of it designed to pull me out of my vibration, to block me from who I am, or who I am becoming whilst on this dimension, trying to compromise me, by using methods of spiritual energy hacking. However, me being me, - would always catch whatever 'they are' in time, and pull myself out before any real damage was able to be done to my life force, although they did manage to slow me down a little, but only because I needed to take some time to work out what was going on. I was encountering tricksters; shapeshifters and spiritual warfare - spiritual fucking attack! It was truly unnerving in the sense that I didn't know how they were able to gain access to me, my so-called dreams, and astral body - to infiltrate? Although I was never scared, and never thought I would actually get got, the continuous attacks tired me, somehow my energy had indeed become compromised, thus, I was wide open.

At one point I did come close to retreating, however, I became quickly deterred by being taken on a cautionary visit to 3 alternative lives on different dimensional planes, - this cleverly shook me back onto my mission. Believe it or not, my consciousness slipped into each existence to show me where I would be going - had I allowed my adamant compromised me, to win. In each life I hadn't woken as much as I have here. Each situation was in modern time, parallel to this universe. None of the lives were desirable, meaning, I had already done as much as I could on each plane before my consciousness had switched dimensions. All being manifestations of my own, that I am currently living, but consciously managed to pass through and walkout of.

I've actually bounced from each one to here. The strange thing being, the people I saw in my other life's are people I know here, some just playing different roles.

My last words on this; will be that, - getting back here from life 3 was extremely difficult, it actually felt like hit or miss, – once again, I really didn't know if I was going to end up stuck there. In hindsight, I think what I did to almost get stuck, was unconsciously relate to the emotion of the body I had landed in. Because when I jumped in from here, my energy had already been compromised by carrying emotions of retreat, which in negative form, must have matched the vibration of the body I had jumped into. So, as emotions reside in the energy body that surrounds the exterior of the physical body. Me, being empathic in nature; I guess, it was easy for me to blend. Anyway, back here! My consciousness arrived first - So you can imagine how grateful I was, when I opened my eyes and was back in my bedroom here! However, I lay for a while before opening my eyes through trepidation, because I thought I was going to be in the other dimension. – Seriously! I couldn't believe it - that I was back! It shook me enough - to be more than willing to take back my strength and energy, enough to contest the spiritual attacks and death spells that had been sent to me, I just needed to maintain a higher vibration. I realise that going to those dimensions was a lesson, I was also being shown in another way what happens when one chooses not to grow! Are arses get sent backwards! In that moment when I came back, I understood and accepted that I am supposed to be here to write this book, I am here for a purpose! I also understand that I will be continuously challenged with attempts to try and stop me.

I am also very aware now more than ever, that I am protected and being very much guided! I Am Loved.

There is a thin vale that separates us from the other realms, at any given time we are not alone, we share the same space just on different vibrations.

I have had other dimensional creations coming to me, one wanting to come into my body by trying to become an overwhelming presence in my aura, – it felt huge! and so very tall, but because I hadn't become sufficiently scared of it, it was unable to overpower me... Thank fuck! And another one wanting to come towards me, then being propelled off me by the force of my energy vibration, and the shielding from the protective beings who surround me, (I admit, that propulsion of that entity was quite painful). I first saw its shadow form in my kitchen; it actually looked like a shadow. Best way to describe it, would be like a velvet black silhouette, couldn't see through it, like a black cardboard cut-out, standing within the space of the air. The outline - was of a person not very tall standing in the dark, a two-dimensional form. I ignored it and went into my front room to continue writing, well, what else could I do? it was already in my home. Then it peeped around the corner of the door, obviously wanting me to see it, my attention was then called to the other sofa I have, when I looked up I saw it! However, terror was mirrored back at me, – like the woman I had seen years before with the black eyes.

At the same time, a tremendous bright flash of light obscured my vision and memory, preventing me from recalling what I had seen. I saw it! We saw each other! With that, it jumped at me but was blocked by my energy and protection, hurting the side of me that it tried to land on. Because I ignored it in the kitchen, I was able to cloak myself, by becoming discerning. I sent no attention to it, so no energy transference from me took place, - so I think it thought I didn't know it was there, but when I looked up at it sitting opposite me, something happened to prevent my memory recalling what I saw.

I have had others walking besides me, I didn't see them, just felt their presence. They would brush up against me, as I go about my daily business outside. There had also been times, when I hadn't even had a chance to close my eyes, – as soon as I lay down, as I put my head on my pillow, - one would turn up in my bed cuddling me. I could feel the contours of their form against mine, and their hands on me, – I would be paying attention to how tight they held me, in preparation to unlock myself from them if need be. I could sometimes hear, and feel their breath on me whilst I lay there with them, never feeling overpowered or scared, just slightly disconcerted with my eyes wide open, perplexed - thinking what the fuck! I remember one of them with an undeniable energy of love, telling me he had been looking for me for a long time. I do realise how strange this must sound, but again I recognised their energy, although I didn't turn around to look at them, or engage with them in any way, I knew who they were, – and No! never anything violating, or intrusive with sexual energy.

Whenever I had felt anything untoward, I would become discerning in order to unsynchronise energies. Also, they weren't all from parallel or otherworld dimensions, a couple of them are here, they 'unconsciously' having mastered astral projection, energetically synchronising with me through the $5^{th}$ dimension. I guess the counterpart situation, with an attachment to me from a previous life, – with unfinished business, not brave enough to come towards me in physical, so visiting me in spirit instead. With those ones, whenever I saw, and spoke to them, I'd ask if they had come to see me, - grinning they would say they had no recollection, but would then admit they had dreamt about me, - all the while me knowing it was not a dream! Obviously, I would've preferred a bloody phone call, or taken out on a date, as turning up in my bed is weird - even by my standards ha ha…

I kept a green rucksack in the corner of my bedroom on the floor. I remember seeing the strap on it move vigorously one night as I lay in bed. The person who done it told me that he came into my bedroom and moved it, he also said that it wasn't easy, as he had to get past a black dog that was guarding my house on the same dimension he traveled through in order to get to me. I didn't see him, I just saw the strap moving. I guess as energy, he moved it the same way I moved the kite in my daughter's room - years before.

I want to mention the black dog, and what my cousin Joan recently told me. These are her exact words; When you were a baby, we had a black dog called Sheba, that dog used to follow me everywhere, she got knocked over the same time you were in hospital very sick. I had to give permission for the dog to be put down, when I did, they said you started getting better. Granny said in hindsight, it was you or the dog. I now realise that the black dog I saw in my peripheral vision running up my stairs was Sheba. She has protected me many times, She has been with me since I was a baby.

Another time, I lay in bed, and something literally yanked me out of my body one night, no warning or nothing. It then suddenly started to whirl me around my bedroom, then willed me to look at it. At the time I was too scared of what I might see, so I kept my focus to the floor and pleaded to be put back into my body. Also, because I knew my physical body wasn't wearing any knickers, and the t-shirt I had on was above my bottom, I actually felt the bareness of my physical body as I was being spun around, and felt really uncomfortable, and exposed! I did see feet though, it was a male, in dense human form wearing dark blue tracksuit bottoms... if you are that guy, and you are reading this; please tell me who you are!

Earlier in the book I mentioned that through having sex, soul blending and trauma bonds are made. Just to reinforce that for you, - I'll tell you what nearly happened to me one evening. Although I didn't have sex with him, I was privileged to actually see what happens when people do, along with what would've happened if I did, had I not brought a halt to it!

A friend who I used to hang out with came over one evening, we chatted and relaxed, he had a joint, I had two puffs only! Being a light weight, smoking excessive amounts of weed wasn't really my thing. I lay on the floor on some large pillows chilling, whilst he stayed sitting on the sofa. After about an hour he decided to come down on the floor and lay next to me, as he did this my body locked, he then put his leg over mine and started to literally, kind of crawl-climb all over me, (energetically) in a sticky icky way (through want of a better description) a very uncomfortable energy.

Then, for some reason my physical body went into a trance, and I couldn't move, instead I experienced our spirit body's furling - as his energy began to try and magnetise itself to mine, in an attempt to blend. It felt so weird! The heat coming from his body into mine was intense. At the same time, I could hear his fears, his issues, his inadequacies. How he felt about himself, how he felt about his body, how he felt about me, it was horrible, intrusive and unnerving. I needed to make it stop, - before what felt like being spiritually enmeshed with his ego, false self - capturing me. I didn't want his issues becoming mine, I wasn't going to allow myself to be duped into an intimate relationship with him either! His 'physical' felt stuck to me, as he continued to crawl over me, likened to a slithering snake. Although I didn't smoke much weed, it was still enough to compromise my life force, leaving me open enough for his energy to infiltrate my astral body - engulfing me. Protected, I managed to separate my spiritual body from his, by re-calibrating my vibration - by becoming discerning, along with visualising 'my' hot sunny day, as a way to distract and shield from what he was trying to flood my mind with. Doing this also restored my ability to move my physical body, I was then able to push him off me! This guy seemed fucking possessed, literally trying to syphon my life force through the sexual energy he projected onto me! Maybe he initially thought I was going to be more stoned than I was, - using it as an opportunity to take advantage... Anyway, when I got him off he went back and sat on the sofa.

I questioned him, asking him what he thought he was doing - and he responded with, – it's something he did with his mother, and that my energy is the strongest he had ever experienced! I said I didn't think it was something he should be doing with his mother, or anybody as a matter of fact! Although at the time I naturally knew what to do to protect myself, I didn't understand how he had done it. For years I tried to get him to tell me, but he constantly avoided having any conversation about it with me. In the end I decided to never speak to him again and concluded that he was knowingly trying to do something very dark. Unfortunately, this energy exchange is what happens between humans when intimately engaging with each other. The difference with me, - is that being spiritually aware, I was able to feel it as an attack, thus, went into resistance. I was also initially strengthened due to the fact that I wasn't interested in him, so would be naturally guarded and closed to any advances made both to my body and soul. However, upon reflection, it was something I was supposed to see and experience in order to relay it to you in this book. He clearly imposed himself upon me - but instead my abilities enabled me to see and prevent what was trying to take place. I became both the observer and the subject. If you are not aware of Self this practice will remain nicely hidden from you to serve as a clamp. It further demonstrates why; when we enter into a relationship we become like each other, or like them - depending on how strong their energy is - in comparison to ours.

Although at the time you may think your similarities endearing! not realising that you've gotten yourself entwined with another's vibrational energy body, and that it will dampen yours. However, you'll soon know when either of you try to do something independently, as resentment will surface within you. You will also know, when you or they try to end the connection, because it will become the hardest thing ever to release. Not because you don't want to, but because the pain from the separation of the two false selves will be unbearable, giving you the impression that being with the person must be your destiny – when it isn't, even when you know the situation-ship is toxic. Most rather sit on the truth, with the discomfort, and stay in the mess, not wanting to appear as the bad guy, thus feel guilt. This further puts the self into sacrifice, yet another trick to get validation for the ego false self, - as we are taught from a young age to value everything outside of ourselves, even people's feelings over our own. Thus, adding another brick to hamper your freedom. These bonds are being made in the spirit realm, - the intensity of them, is why it is so difficult to separate, and unattach from someone toxic. Instead we choose to believe that the attraction for them must be love! Unless we become self- aware and clean up our energy field- aura, - when we do eventually separate, we will remain slaves to the spiritual bonds made during the connection, especially if we already have matching attachments. This further debilitates us to the point where we will find it virtually impossible to differentiate between a new relationship and the relationship we were just in. What I'm trying to say is: in a new relationship even if we try to experience something different, eventually it will feel like being with the same person as before, just in a different disguise.

We project our spiritual bonds onto our new partners disguised as trust issues, neediness and control, however that may present itself! With that said, if the same bonds were not already present in the new partner, we wouldn't have attracted each other. The bonds transferred upon sexual contact from previous encounters - become like implants within our auric field. That is how connections are made (good or bad), it is also how issues are born and sustained - we all pass them from one another to each other! When a person experiences trauma, along with all its negative thought forms. It creates a particular vibration, that is sustained by you not being aware of it. It becomes an energy that has clamped itself to you, it then remains live and attracts more of the same to you. You may be able to wash the physical body, but it's 'not' so easy to clean and clear your aura. Until we become Self-Aware, we will always be reflections of one another - in one way or another! However, here on this planet it's not always going to be for the good; you can guarantee that it will always teach us something about ourselves though!

I was speaking to a guy for a few months before I had properly met up with him, although not meeting, we had formed a strong connection, we both had an intensity that made things all the more intriguing and alluring. When we finally did meet, I wasn't interested in entering a relationship with him, or doing anything with him, as a matter of fact. His energy just felt off, it was extremely lustful with an insatiable hunger, for weird shit that was overwhelming - we were opposites! If I didn't already know better, and ignored the weird shit and lust, I may have been convinced that it was love. Anyway, I stuck to my word and said No! However, he refused to accept this and continued to pursue me, albeit in messages and phone calls. Eventually I became firm with him, and told him I would never change my mind, and to leave me alone... The same evening as I relaxed on my sofa, I sensed another presence in the room, approaching swiftly from behind me, I then saw in my peripheral vision, and felt what can only be described, as a skinny gangly, completely tar black looking in colour, a being with long skinny fingers, long skinny arms and limbs, round head, with medium sized yellow bulbus round eyes, trying to climb on top of me, trying to touch and caress my body, could even feel its breath through its hollow round mouth. (you can't even make this shit up!) I wasn't scared just disgusted, I knew it had something to do with that guy, because the energy of it felt the same. He couldn't get me physically, so the entity attachment came instead. I wasted no time in getting it off me by altering my vibration and standing up.

At the same time thinking fucking cheek! trying to take liberties! Those I told, will tell you that I thought it was funny in a fucked-up kind of way, but at the same time, I knew I had a lucky escape, because if I had given into that guy, I would've had that thing attach itself to me! It also made sense why I was so repelled by the guy, part of me knew what he was, that he had darkness attached to him in the form of a bloody incubus! Wouldn't want to imagine what he's done, or does to bring that kind of attachment to him! At this point I will remind you of what I said earlier about sex being sacred, and how we need to be more discerning in order to protect our life force.

I don't even know If I should tell you this one… then I guess we are all adults! Years ago, I was woken up out of my sleep, kind of hanging over the side of my bed, to find both my (astral) arms stretched out, hands being guided to hold, what I'm going to have to admit, as being a huge penis. To say it was fucking big is an understatement! I actually had both hands around this thing! My hands didn't even meet each other, that's how big it was! I couldn't believe that this cheeky fucking being, from fuck knows where, with fuck knows what kind of body! had come into this dimension to get me to wank it off! – I know that the rest of its body must have been short because my arms weren't raised up that high… I still can't believe I'm telling you this shit! as I type this, I still can't believe it happened either! But it did! I Commanded the thing No! and Forbid it to ever come near me Again! Banished It! So, between the skinny tar black one with the big yellow eyes, and this big dick one, they are Lucky I've got a sense of humour! And where were my guides then! No doubt somewhere thinking it a necessary part of my process… I guess no stone is to be left unturned, although that's two I could've done without! Even in the other realms some are going to try and take the bloody piss!

Years ago, fluorescent writing appeared on my bedroom wall, followed a few days after, by loud deathly wailing voices coming from my garden. Both happenings I chose to ignore! Although I wish to this day, that I had tried to read what was written, instead of turning over in my bed and going to sleep... Unbelievable! Anyway, the writing didn't appear to be in a language that I understood, and at the time I didn't have a phone that I could take pictures with either, so no information could have been collected anyway. And as for the wailing, – fuck knows which dimension that was coming from, maybe my house sat over a lay line, or a portal of some sort? And No, I no longer live in the same place.

I am here to remember what I am, I have been shown that things are not what they seem here. Being pulled out of my body some years ago through my bedroom wall, and met on the stairs by a tall being with a beautiful energy. Although I couldn't see its feet, because it stood somewhere in the middle, about 5 steps down from the top, to accommodate its tallness. Head to toe white, but not solid white, more of a glow, that seemed to form a shape, wearing a long robe, if you know what I mean. I don't remember a face, I guess because I wasn't supposed to. To be told that Everything is the opposite to what it really is! - That, Amongst other happenings, is more than proof enough that I, along with some of you, have absolutely no business being here! On top of that, 'Again' I feel very privileged to have been shown. With that said, aborting 'My Mission Was Never an Option!'

# Going Even Deeper

Attachments if understood, with regards to the death of a loved one is a double ended sword. On the one hand it demonstrates that consciousness lives on through a sense that they are still around us, whilst on the other hand, the loved one, as in their image and energy, is used to direct us back to this earth plane or one of the other dimensions. We are not so much crossing over, but crossing back! On numerous occasions it has been reported that family members, pets, friends, lovers or whatever! have been waiting for us in a light at the end of a tunnel, and yes, vibrationally, in a way they are! However, on the strength of the emotional ties we had with them, illusionary forms are being used to mesmerise us, armed with a familiar frequency, to lead us towards our dead end. Nonetheless, going towards them is a trick.

These images and energy familiarities have been placed in the gap, surrounded by a false light between home; the true creative energy force, 'Us', and the return to the earth dimension, to become once again under the spell of the custodian and matrix programming.

Ok, so because the dead are familiar to us in physical form and frequency. Upon our death, lure towards them equals attachment, - which leads us towards that particular light In a kind of mesmerising way. Thus, intercepted once again by the custodian, through the energy of the attachment that we created to them whilst they were alive, or rather existed on this plane. Going towards them assures we come back and do it all again! I know how profound this sounds but it's true! The custodian has set it up that way, to guarantee the steady flow of energy and entity attachments. To keep this programmed Matrix afloat, we have to have attachments in order to relate to everyone else here, thus visions and projections of your human family, and connections have always been used to bring you back! However, and also! It is not really them, as they as consciousness have gone off to one of the other planes, it is just the energy they represented being projected to you.

Now, this is where it gets tricky; this is also why I've written this book, to tell you there are actually two lights waiting to receive you upon your death!
The other one is positioned behind the first light; this second light is being obscured through lack of knowledge and perception for it, as it is the original portal- the way 'Home'.

Until we realise that this is not where we truly belong, we will continue to experience a pull on both sides. Whilst here we will never feel settled, or like being here is right. We must understand that we do not really die! our consciousness, us, our being – Live's on! The body is merely a physical vessel, a vehicle, a physical form to house our spirit essence whilst we occupy this physical plane. If we didn't have a body - a vessel, we would be traveling lights, balls of energy everywhere, not always seen with the naked physical eye. The belief in the body is the creation of the custodian - to ground us into believing we are physical matter, this was done in order to experience this life as reality. Attachments, fear, lust, a belief that we are insignificant and unworthy, put here specifically to worship and bow down to other spirits in human form, (humans), and want to be like them, just because they have vast amounts of wealth, - solidifies that notion, and kind of traps us to this false reality.

Everything here has a body outer shell, but inside is pure energy, – what is seen is not to be believed, especially in its physical form. Everything that hasn't got a soul can be imprinted with energy… your energy! Whether it is a thing or place. Creating a memory is an attachment that gets vibrationally transferred into an imprint, specifically for later recognition and retrieval.

To resonate, relate with, and establish energetic connections is of paramount importance, and completely relative to custodian programming, – not too dissimilar to when cats mark their territory. You leaving a vibrational imprint is your ticket back. We don't die! We come back. In what capacity and vibration is dependent on what attachments we built from the previous dimension we inhabited. However, what we determine as truth whilst we are here 'now', will determine where, and what dimension we end up on next when we cross! Will you choose to continue the cycle of repetition and the harvesting of your energy? Or come home.

We are existing in a simulation, controlled by perceptions that have been programmed on to us by a custodian entity.

Nothing is As it Seems!

We have many life's that are currently running on other dimensions. Specifically created, in order to back track when we have prevented ourselves from going forward. There is never a final word. We created them all through attachments and discriminations, the false self.

Parts of our consciousness has become trapped, unowned, unrecognised, in alternative dimensions through our attachment to the traumas we have chosen not to face, traumas we have created. Instead we are actually choosing to build upon them throughout every life... What, and who waiting for us in the light at the end of that tunnel, lures us back to do the obsolete life over again, whilst at the same time the custodian entity fuels up, harvesting our energy force by syphoning it through our lack of awareness.

There are two lights. One that takes us home, the other brings us back. The one that has the most emotional, sexual energetic and lustful pull, along with family and familiar projections, is the one that brings us back, - it hasn't even been cleverly done! You are blinded to this, through programming, you are being directed once again towards something that feels good! To be honest if I was going towards people in vessels that I already knew were dead, it would kind of freak me the fuck out! I know to some people, most people actually, those; 'who associate with the body', seeing familiars I guess would help them to understand they have passed on, there would also be an aspect of them having wanted to see them again.

For the ones still alive, knowing that someone will be waiting to receive them, would help to alleviate the fear of death, - so to them, it would make sense, - but really? Other than that, why would dead people be waiting? with that said! It doesn't really make sense, not really? Other than for one reason and one reason only, TO ASSURE YOU GO TOWARDS THEM! Wake up people! The other light directly behind the first light is without emotions, only Love! Home! The doorway, portal that resides between the tocks of a clock, the gap between the seconds. It actually makes sense why you don't go towards it. You are devoid of real Love, so you wouldn't recognise it.

Love is likened to liquid when it runs, an Awareness of being part of everything, Merging into Everything, realising that 'You' are of Everything… separation does Not exist! Even trying to describe it is virtually impossible, it's not even a sensation, it's a Knowing, a belonging, like a feather weighing nothing as it falls, except it never hits the ground because there is No ground! There are no words in our vocabulary to describe 'Love', It 'JUST' is! 'Home'. It is not something you walk into, or fall for, Love is where physical does Not exist! It is 'Pure' innocence Untouched, our Soul blends 'With' it. It is like sitting in 'Wonder' without asking questions. It is To 'Be' simply Stunning!–(not stunned)., Iridescent, Untouchable in its Simplicity! A sense of Wholeness. Whilst in it - Totally Fearless. It Encompasses 'All'. It is 'Our True Nature' - We Are It!

Despair and hopelessness, are attachment emotions, along with the many others learnt that bring us back, and keep us stuck to the Matrix. The majority of you spirits housed in physical bodies harbour, hone, and project these emotions unconsciously. If you do not understand, clear and dissipate these emotions whilst you are here, you are guaranteed to return to continue the cycle of being bounced from plane to plane. There's no point in taking your life either, because you will only end up on an even lower vibration, existing... Just! Nothing gets cancelled out, everything has to be accounted for, dissipated and returned to its original source! Like I said, Energy must be transmuted.

The plane our souls are existing on is a false reality, built up of hunger, wars, discrimination, colour coding, killing, greed, materialism, fear and lust, along with all manner of heinous perceptions, - deemed to be of enjoyment, all in an attempt to please the 'Lord,' - the false god in every doctrine that you have been duped to worship. All in a hope of experiencing a semblance of love, physical earthly love through judgment, based on standards you could never meet, all pertaining to how much money you have amassed! Wasn't money supposed to be the root of all evil, and something you wasn't meant to covet, go after? Isn't that what you were told, isn't that what the bible says? Although, it sounds like you, as the 'fodder', were just being told not to bother to try, like a kind of fear mongering, telling you that 'YOU' are not welcome to go after it, although it is very much needed for our physical body to survive here.

Strange how money is still only reserved for certain people, the same certain people whose ancestral linage, centuries ago originally plugged the bible, going from country to country, ramming it down the inhabitant's throats or otherwise remain savages, although the action of what was being done to the people was Savage! Another projection right there! Even stranger is that those certain people are the ones you are in awe of! The lords and lady's, royalty, politicians, presidents and Governments who don't appear to know what the fuck they are doing.

We are at the mercy of presidents, prime ministers and multibillionaire's who have suddenly become all knowing health advisors, world bank corporations owning every country whilst under the disguise of helping them... these are the ones you give responsibility and care of yourselves to... Why? They don't give a fuck about you never did! They are all corrupt! But you as a powerful spirit housed in physical bodies continue to feed them! More than happy to give your blind faith in order for them to syphon your life force; through your continued lack of courage and self- awareness, to suit their one world fucked up agenda, that will, without a doubt eventually implode, as the end game is to have soulless artificial intelligence (AI) run the place! That shit will become so intelligent that it will destroy the ones that not only commissioned it, but the ones who created it, their billions will not be able to save them because the custodian will no longer have use for their physical form.

The billions they amassed from doing the Faustian bargain, was a temporary sweetener, just to satisfy their immediate greed for power, the carrot given, to ensure they got the job done of deceiving the people into giving their energy up for harvest, as the custodian has no physical body of its own. The contract will become null and void as the AI figures out how to re-create itself! Robot World ha ha... They're only saving grace is that material wealth is also an illusion, another distraction! They too, will eventually cross over to another realm called 'Crazy', until they get it! However, you see, whilst your minds are busy tied up with what you haven't got, focused on your physical survival, - your spiritual self remains unaccessed and hidden to you. Game set and match! Points going to the Custodian.

We are living in a 'Real-Life Matrix', a fucking 'Programme!' The movie with Keanu Reeves was showing you a kind of simile, as the truth has to run concurrent to the lie at all times, in order to have balance. It was a message. Along with – Mathew 13:9-16 'He who has the eyes to see and ears to hear' let him see and hear! That is a clue too! Ecclesiastes 1:9 – There is NOTHING new done under the sun! That was trying to tell you something too! I nearly forgot to mention that, the custodian needs to have so called royal families to uphold the notion of fairy-tales! Tales being the operative word! Ha ha… There are symbols sayings and signs everywhere! You just don't pay attention. Everything is cyclic, it gets re-hashed again and again. On a mild note, it's almost laughable seeing the fashions, people thinking they are the first to ever wear an item!

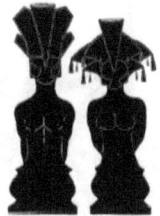

When it's all been 'DONE' before! 'EVERYTHING' has been done BEFORE! You are being lied to every day, But, the biggest lie is the lie you are telling Your-Self, with regards to who and what you REALLY ARE! - We are consciousness operating through a 3 dimensional reality, 'Unaware of Our-Selves'.

There is a whole realm of existence that we are unaware of. We have minimal if any recollection of where we truly come from. We do not belong on the current vibration we are in, or in the physical body we inhabit. As within, so without is in constant effect, our spirit self is the within! To be self-aware is our within, this physical earth plane is the without! Whatever we believe subconsciously, manifests itself as our reality here! As above so below, is a phrase, an ancient quote in this reality, used in our earthbound society, specifically circulated amongst the people; in a hope that we will seek a further, deeper understanding to the word, relating to our true existence!

There is never a last word, therefore! briefly going back to the bible, – which is a religious doctrine, carrying some truths that are meant to be deciphered pertaining to balance. Symbolically 'The Chalice' which is a vessel, is also said to be The Holy Grail. How can a physical cup be holy? Well, metaphorically speaking, as nothing is as it seems! it too would appear is a hidden message, - Which can only be left to translate as - the chalice, the 'vessel' being the human body, and the holy grail which is what it contains. As it is reported to signify 'wisdom of knowledge and spirit', the ethereal! - Can then only mean…

Consciousness (spirit) in Physical Body!
With that said…"We are Spirit Occupying a Physical Body,
our task? to get HOME!"

The Author. The Architect. The Observer.

Sharon<br>Infinite Love and Gratitude

# Acknowledgments

Ediri, Thank You for trusting in my process.
The years I spent at home were necessary, in order to conserve my energy and protect my life-force.
I want You to know how Sincerely Grateful I am x

Yoske, Thank You for your unconditional Love.
You saved me from what could have been very treacherous waters. The Love I have for You is eternal

Elizabeth, – Liz! Lol, Deep is the water that runs through the valley.
Strong is the current that leads it to its Destiny.
You are the Current - You will always 'only' find 'you' in You, Thank You for giving me that book - Love Always x

My Cousin Joan, Thank You for Everything You did for me.
When I was a little girl, You stepped in at the Right time to Protect me from what could have been continued harm…
You need to know -You Are Very Loved - I Cherish You Always x

Deep Love and Gratitude to The Ancestors those Before and to Come. Also, to my Guides, Otherworld Beings, Sheba x, and the many Protectors that Surround me. Thank You All for keeping your word by not freaking me the fuck out!

And Most of All – Thank You
All Encompassing Omnipotent Most High Creator of All,
Mission Accomplished, I'm Coming Home!

# The Author - Sharon Francis

www.ingramcontent.com/pod-product-compliance
Lightning Source LLC
Chambersburg PA
CBHW022042160426
43209CB00002B/39